I Remember Alice

A Story of Her Family, An Unusual Courtship, and Counseling of The Spirit

Palma Richardson

A BIOGRAPHY OF MY MOTHER

Dear Bessie & Earl,
Love the years
we've spent time.
It's always been fun
time. Hope you enjoy
and God Bless you.
Love, Palma
3/27/12

ISBN: 978-0-615-38229-6

Library of Congress Control Number: 2010930994

Printed in the United States of America

To order copies of this book, email: palmareia@gmail.com

Cover and interior design by www.tothepointsolutions.com

To those who knew and loved Alice.

Alice's Family Tree

1st Generation	**2nd Generation**	**Spouse**	**3rd Generation**
Martha Jones James W. Halstead	Myrtle	*Joseph MacNamee*	Vivian
			Gertrude
			Dorothy
			Bob*
			Joe
			Jim*
			Mary Jayne
			Patrick
	Tom	*Mary Hayden*	Gladys*
			Evelyn
	James		
	Alice	*Owen Tredway*	Janis*
			Palma
	George	*Loraine Greenwald**	Marilyn
	Clara	*Ole Severson*	Sally
			John
	Charles	*Jackie Madigan**	Tom
			Nancy
			Bob
			Mary
			Tim
	John (Jack)	*Madeline*	

* Interviewed for this book

Alice's Family Tree

Spouse	***4th Generation***	***Spouse***	***5th Generation***
John Dudash	Joan*	*Robert Mott*	Sarah
			John
Alvin Reffruschinni	RaeLynn	*John Wilson*	Alicia
			Tiffany
			Julia
	Owen		
	David		
	Bridget	*David Spector*	Kenneth
			Louis
			Kyla
	Katie		
Kurt Luscombe			
Kermit Richardson	Kenneth Grant	*Deanna Radcliffe*	
		Sarah Braiman	Owen
			Greta
			Holly
	Eric	*Patrizia Scaramella*	
	Kermit Will (Willy)	*Martha Strom*	
		Kelsey Brown	
	Karla	*Randy Velikan*	
Larry Hooton	Shawn	*Kristi Freng*	
	Shane		
Mary Rajala	Zachary		
	Lance		

Contents

Acknowledgments

I HAD NO IDEA THAT WRITING A BOOK would be such a huge undertaking when I started writing in 1994. I wrote down five pages and then was at a standstill. I discovered I didn't know much about my mother's family. So I decided to interview people who had known my Grandma and Grandpa.

The people that I interviewed became part of the story as they all remembered different aspects of Alice and her family. Alice's sisters in law, Aunt Jackie Halstead and Aunt Loraine Halstead, cousins Bob and Jim MacNamee, Gladys Dudash and daughter Joan Mott, sister Janis and cousin Tredway Haglund on my father's side. Mother's friend Brynhild Mitchell lifelong resident of Munising was very helpful because she remembered Alice in her younger years, as did Bernice Williams. Allyn Roberts and Elaine Hodge gave a professional glimpse of Mother's work and their own experience with her therapy.

Then I dug out the letters. My daughter Karla got me started on these by organizing them chronologically. Then Janis provided me with journals that I hadn't known about and the story started to emerge.

The experience of editing was new for me. With the help of my sister Janis, and Marty Strom, we reread and I rewrote, many times. Amos Mauie, Barbara Disborough, and Frances Ogle offered suggestions and ideas from their own experience. Stephanie Mills was particularly helpful in being a support. As an experienced writer she was able to guide me over the humps and valleys of writing a book.

Jim Clumpner, helped by being a friend of Alice and mine, the artist of the "trees", and general support throughout this project. Katie Reffruschinni came to my aid when I needed a drawing of the loghouse and farm. She had special insight into these old buildings.

At this time I was looking for pictures of the building at the "old farm" and John Severson looked through Clara's shoeboxes and came up with such neat old pictures that I decided to find more, from Janis and my collections, and insert them into the story.

When I decided to insert pictures in the text, I needed more help and Sue Sudekum gave me many ideas in beginning the book setup. Then Mary Jo Zazueta came into the project and has done a wonderful job of designing and editing the book with its many aspects.

Last but not least, Ed Vespa, my partner, put up with me being engrossed in this book for fifteen plus years of our winter vacations in Florida. He also did a lot of listening as I sounded out ideas. So thanks to all who participated in this project, whether I remembered you here or not.

Introduction

THIS STORY IS ABOUT ALICE, MY MOTHER. One summer in the 1940s when I was ten or so a girlfriend and I, looking for something to do, climbed the stairs into the attic of our house. It was a partially finished attic with floor boards, a window at each end of the space but the ceiling rafters were low and unfinished. We browsed around in the dust, looking at old pictures in frames, discarded antique chairs, and a pile of very old magazines. There were *Saturday Evening Posts* and *Ladies Home Journals* from the early 1900s which seemed like a real archeological find. Then we spied a shoebox. Upon opening it up we discovered it full of letters from my father to my mother in the 1920's and 30's. Though I never read any of them at that time, I always knew they were there.

When my mom passed away in April of 1987, my sister Janis and I went through her bedroom shortly after the funeral. It was so painful, we decided to go through the rest of the house at a later date. We set the date for June, with nicer weather and some healing time. Since Janis would be coming all the way from Tucson, Arizona and would be there for only a week, we focussed on the main house, leaving the attic and basement to me for another time. So, as we went through the house, everyone else was concerned that we should save all of her papers, notes, and files of case histories. I wasn't much interested at that time. I did save the letters from the attic though.

So it was in the later 1990's that I decided someone should write down some of the family's history, and that someone seemed to be me. When I started writing, I realized that I really didn't know that much. Now all the notes and letters and journals that had been saved became important to me also. All of Alice's generation was gone so I then decided to interview the older cousins, who told stories about their parents, and Grandma and Grandpa. I also talked to the only two surviving spouses of her brothers. In my mind, I would also have to include the story of her work, and her development of her theories. So I also interviewed those who knew her in that way.

I've tried to keep several threads throughout; that of her birth family, of her married family and of her quest towards developing her own psyche and spiritual self.

Since that time, this story has told itself as I recalled what she told me, what others remembered, excerpts from her journals, and the letters I found in the attic that summer day long ago. This journey through time has been long and hard, but fun.

Part One

1909 to 1948

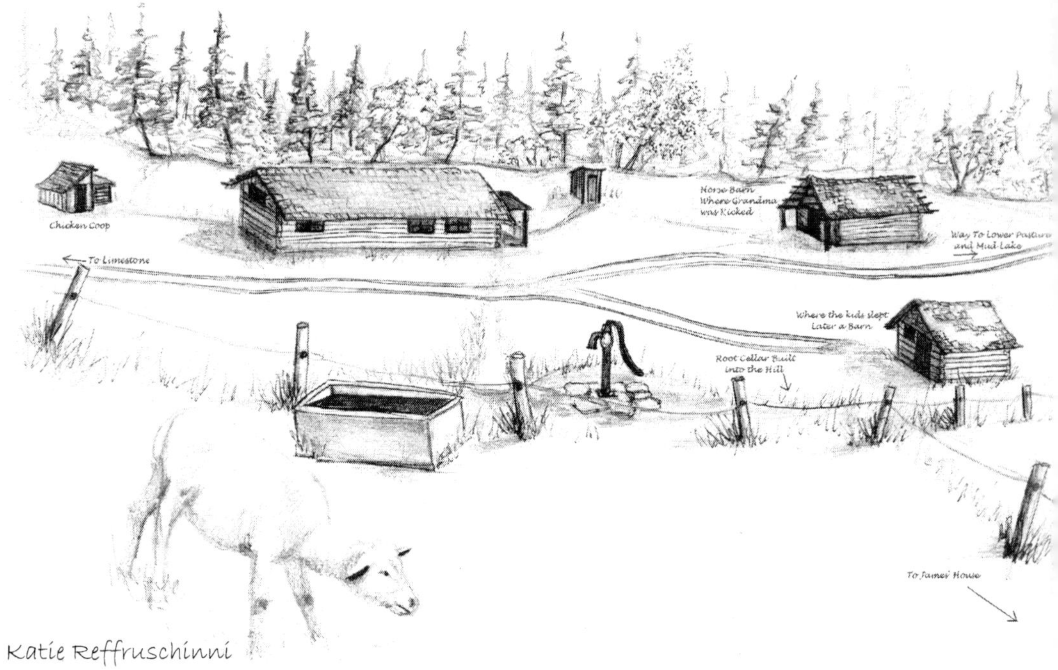
Chicken Coop
To Limestone
Horse Barn
Where Grandma
was Kicked
Way To Lower Pastur
and Mud Lake
Where the kids slept
Later a Barn
Root Cellar Built
into the Hill
To James' House
Katie Reffruschinni

Katie Reffruschinni

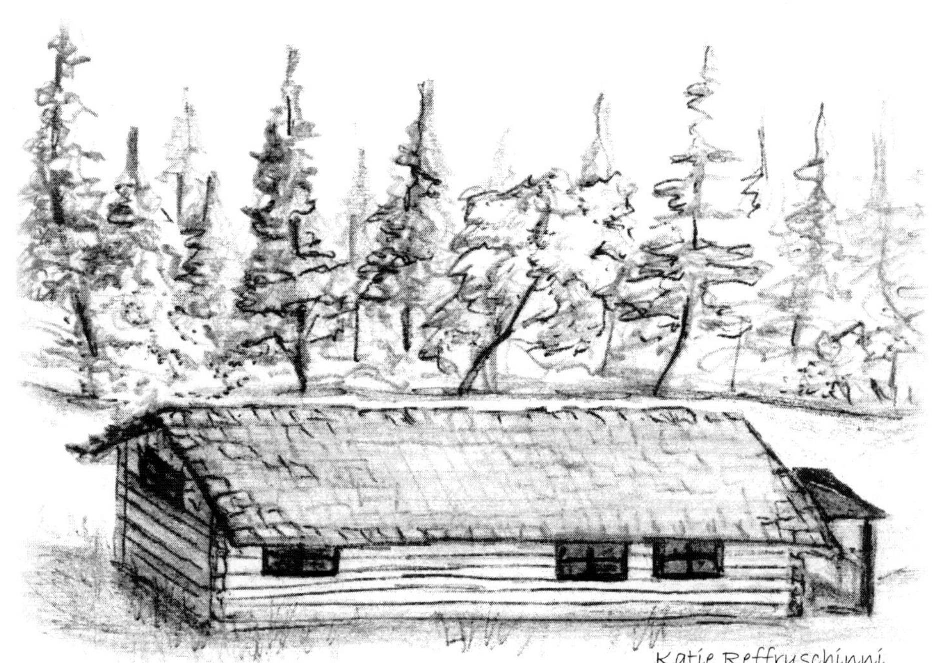

The Farm

SHE GREW UP IN A ONE ROOM cabin in the north woods of Michigan. It was set below a hill in a grassy plain where I vaguely remember a rickety barn, a root cellar and a hand water pump on a little rise facing the cabin. The patchy whitewash on the exterior of the buildings gave it a derelict look. Coming to visit we would leave a beautiful three bedroom home in Munising and drive twenty miles or so. Mother would say, "Watch for Old Joes." "Old Joes" was the local tavern in the village of Limestone, Michigan, and it was the landmark for the road to the farm.*

We would turn there onto a dirt road, go a couple of miles and then turn off again on a two rut road. It was exciting to come up over the last rise and see the farm. There was usually a dog, some cats and in the earlier days, even a cow which was named Daisy as I recall.

> *Janis* [my sister]: Uncle Jack, and Grandma, they had a device that went under the collar of a cow that went over or under the fence. Susie jumped over the fence and Daisy went under the fence. They had a thing sticking up on Daisy's collar so she couldn't get under the fence and a thing sticking down on Susie's collar so she couldn't go over the fence. So, we'd go out in the morning in the wet dew into the woods. I could never keep up with Grandma in the woods. She was in her seventies and I couldn't keep up with her. She'd be chargin' along hollerin' "SUUUUU Bossy, SUUUUU Bossy", calling the cows to come home and be milked.

I remember walking in to the smell of home-baked bread, soup simmering on the wood stove and the smell of rutabaga and cabbage pervasive through it all. Grandma would say, "How about a piece of homemade bread?" So we'd sit down at the big kitchen table and layer butter and sugar on our fresh bread.

---

*Old Joe's burned down twice. Mother and her siblings hated it not only because they hated drink but because the building had once been their school. It burned the second time the night Uncle George died. We are all sure that he had a hand in it!

Grandma and Janis playing with kittens.

Janis: I remember the log house very clearly, I stayed out there, and it wasn't all that little!! The main room was about 15 x 20. There was room for the big range [wood cookstove], cupboards, a large trestle table, probably a bed/couch. Then there was another room. That was the bedroom but it wasn't as big. It was a two room log cabin. The bedroom was big enough for a pot-bellied stove and a big bed. I asked, "How did all those people sleep in there?"

The baby slept with them, and the youngest child slept across the bottom of the bed. And the only thing I know about sleeping arrangements was when they all had mumps or measles at once, hammocks were hung from the ceiling so they could all be in bed at once. [Jan laughs]; I don't know where they all slept. They probably had more beds then 'cause they were all grown up when I stayed there and they didn't need so many beds. I don't even know where they slept then. I didn't pay much attention. Maybe the bedroom was bigger, maybe there were two beds. I said, "Where did you sleep when you stayed

Gladys and Prince.

Grandma on the farm.

James with plough horses.

(l to r): Clara, their dad, and Alice.

Grandma in Munising *(1933)*.

there?" Well they made me a bed. Uncle James took a couple of boards and so there was a bed about the size of a cot, filled it up with hay and set it up in the main room. I stayed out there with Mary Jayne and Jimmy [our cousins], and I don't know where they slept. [Perhaps they stayed in the barn where I've been told they had bunks. Aunt Jackie says, "Charles remembered running from the barn to the house in bare feet in the snow!!"]

Those things didn't bother me as a child, but I know there was a pot-bellied stove in the bedroom. I remember when I stayed out there when I was about 12, we went out raspberry picking all morning. Grandma said, " Now, you can those raspberries while I take a nap,and this is how you can raspberries." She went to bed and took a nap and I canned the raspberries. Mother was right about that, Grandma was really good at teaching kids things. So there was room for a pot-bellied stove and cupboards with shelves up above, and of course in those days people didn't have all the clothes. You know, they had one change of clothes, they didn't need all that space.

I don't think I was ever in the bedroom, I never stayed overnight. By the time I came along and was big enough to remember much they had moved from Limestone out to the farm at Fox.

Gladys Dudash [Tom's daughter]: There were two big rooms. The big front room had a cookstove and a big table. We'd go in the bedroom and we'd hear them out there talking politics. The bedroom was piled high with papers and magazines. When we'd visit we (my sister Evelyn and I) loved to ride Prince [the horse] bareback. We rode out in the woods and would have to duck branches. Grandma would take us fishing in a little rowboat at Mud Lake. It had stumps sticking up all over it, but we did catch little fish—we might have thrown them back. Grandma would feed us venison that she had canned and she'd take us picking blueberries or wild strawberries at the edge of the field. I remember her always busy and smiling, with her blue eyes and curly white hair.

Bob McNamee [Myrtle's son]: That little cabin they lived in was pretty much two rooms. There was a lumberjack style kitchen. The roof came down close to the ground and of course with no insulation, in the winter there were these big thick icicles right to the ground. It was a log cabin with newspaper chinking.

Grandma was an excellent cook. She didn't have much to cook with back in those days but they'd [the Government] give needy people some food back then during the Depression, just before FDR was voted in to be President. The flour they'd give them was like the whole grain kind. She'd mix that with white flour and she'd make the best bread you ever did taste. She could make almost anything taste good. She was really a gainful person. She'd take me out fishin' there in Mud Lake. We'd get a boat from that old fellow that used to live down there and what we did was row out where it was deep to fish. They built little canals out behind the dam so you could get out where it was deep to fish. There were quite a few bass in there. The dam was built there for power.

Mother had seven living brothers and sisters. Two others had died as infants. As there was not much money made, life was pretty sparse for the family. It seemed though that learning was a priority. The one room school house was three miles away, and it later became Old Joe's. When Grandpa's horse and wagon were not available for transportation, the kids walked to school. I can imagine wading through the snow in winter, slushing around in mud when spring came and the snows were melting, and walking home drenched by the autumn rains. On the other hand, walking home or to school maybe hearing birds sing, picking ripe berries along the road, feeling the warm sun and looking at wildflowers blooming at the edge of the woods or in the meadow.

I remember hearing about this dedication to school, and part of that story was how they used to only have cold potatoes to take for their lunches!!! I understand that they were hot from the oven and kept their hands warm on the way to school, then ate them cold at lunchtime. Imagine the fun though when Grandpa would drive them to school with the team of horses and wagon. If it was winter and the snow was deep, the horses would be hitched to a sleigh. Later when no bus was provided for his children, Grandpa ran to become a School Board member,

Jackie Halstead [Charlie's wife]: When Charles was a little boy, he went off to school when he was in first grade. One day the teacher assigned a story to read during bell time (you know, before the bell rang). Anyway, it was "Chicken Little." Charles came to this word and didn't quite know what it was, So he went up to the teacher and said, "Is this Chicken Little thought back or Chicken Little turned back?" She said, "Charlie Halstead, you go back to your seat and figure it out!!" So he figured out what he thought. So school started and they were reading the story. When it came to that part of the story and each child was taking a turn to read she said, "Just a minute we're going to have Charlie read this part." So he stood up and very laboriously read, "Chicken Little thought back." The teacher ran over and grabbed the book out of his hands and pounded him over the head with it. She told him how stupid he was that he got the word wrong. So he sat down and packed up all of his things and never said a word and got up to leave. She said, "Charlie Halstead, where do you think you're going?" He just looked at her and he walked home. When he got home his mother said, "Why are you here?" He told her what had happened and she said, "You don't have to go back to school, I'll teach you here at home." So he was a first-grade dropout. His mother taught him at home the rest of the year. The next year when he went back to school they tested him. He did so well they put him in third grade. So Grandma was an early homeschooler.

Jim McNamee: Mom [Myrtle] went to school one day and they were told to stand up and pledge allegiance to the flag. She had trouble with her hearing, and so she didn't hear what they were supposed to do. She was busy coloring. The teacher came over and whacked her. My mom went home and never went back until she went to high school. Grandma, she taught them at home.

I remember Grandma as a diminutive lady with white curly hair and a slight limp. She had a resigned air about her as if—"This is how it is, so I'll just accept it"—Her most distinguishing physical feature I remember when I was a child of 4 or 5 was a prominent Adam's apple [a goiter from a lack of iodine earlier in her life], which bobbed up and down all the while she talked. When she talked, which was seldom, I was fascinated.

The stories about Grandma from her children were about her great abilities to be at one with nature, her great sense of humor, [very dry as as I remember] and her gentleness. The woods was home to Grandma and the plants, her friends. She knew the berry patches and the nettles danger areas. Each tree and wildflower had a name. These are things she passed on to her children and my mother passed on to me, somewhat diluted, I might add.

This poem, written by Alice in the 1960s, tells a lot about Grandma.

SHE

A crystaline clear spring, ever renewing
from its source. Back bent
But glory in her face; gnarled hands,
broken nails and worn; with gentleness
That helped Cat birth her kits; with kind skill
plucked the quills from Lucky's nose;
Held new chicks. She is as she is, true centrality,
our reality. Each found her profound

The Farm

In wisdom, his model, his goal, sought his role
of Life in her virtue. She taught as she ought,
By living. We caught her spirit, and today

Express, say in our lives the part of her
we came to be. Her determination
Became Clara's; doors and gates open at her will;
Georges estates of service, beauty,
Show clearly her indefatigability. James'
key to happiness her immediacy. Tom
Measures his attainment by her simplicity,
rich in valor, talent, worth,
Charles' endowment from birth has been
her unobtrusive goodness; mine her ideals,
Her way of finding in each her fellowman,
quality; John speaks her Spit Wit.

Born poor, pain poor, her poverty paved past
molded her, held her fast;
Straightened, chastened, stated her boundaries
to the last. Yet she lived richly,
Each day she reached and in reaching
found values that stressed her strength.
She lifted us, unshackled us, freed us to be
as rich as she. She lived each notion
That she set in motion, each thought she taught
and each day thought anew. She
Burned old bridges daily; we marveled how
fresh structures of mind put to action

Grew. Possibility became Actuality. No milk?
She somehow earned a cow. No flour? No bread?
A field was cleared, turned with plow; no spuds?
no problem; she coaxed the earth with
Sweated brow. No fruit? Plains, swamps, fields
yield berries, endow. No money? No matter,
Christmas is the candled balsam lit while
we sit around and sing the songs
We know, lamps turned low. No gifts?, We like
just remembering the day when
Jesus lay in a manger of hay just like Danny's,
warm with the body and breath of donkeys.

Molasses taffy pulled and stretched sweet our
memories etched; stories read from
Books hoarded, accorded us with pleasures
and treasures and unknown dividends.
No school. We lived too far to walk. Slate
and chalk, brown paper torn from
Ends and tags of paper bags displayed
our verbs and nouns, maps of countries,
Seas, states, and towns, and drills
of words, preparing us for weekly
Spelldowns, along with number races and
geography games of names and places.

Neighbors found her heart and soul of
each community. They might cheat,
Beat up on one another, wrangle, steal, or
back bite; but in her they found their

Worth, set forth to match charity
with hers. In-laws called her Saint while
Yet among them; turned their children to
her, who found in her courage, their courage
To be themselves. "Dear little Grandma
has the world by the tail."
She held for searchers, the cup,
The Holy Grail.

Cliches were not cliches but enhanced; her
spirit danced and sang for
Love of life. She whistled away her worries,
crossed bridges when she came
Upon them; said, "People respond to what
you see in them;" "Give the kids a
Chance to grow up;" "Who can be good when
spoken of as bad;" "Stand between no
Man and his God;" "Conduct yourself in such a
way that you need defer to no one;"
"When one door shuts, another opens;" "Adversity
is a good teacher but gentleness a

Better one;" "Stars show brightest
on a dark night."
As Harvard bred Thoreau, she studied art of
beingness; chose Nature's natural
Stress to find a life of simpleness. As Martha
she is thrust without means to test
Her philosophy, which she proved with her
gentility its basic reality.

I Remember Alice

The simple life is best. She added
zest to everything she did, we did,
Spared us no painful experience; led us to see
insecurity promotes maturity.

She knew Nature's subtleties,
mysterious ways. Few days
Passed that she did not share with us
these intrigues. Snow prints of
Brownbunny's dare to a pair of shrewd coyote minds,
fast feet; oriole's hammock hung,
Swung high from the elm; the sharp tail's
quadrilles; whippoorwill's still
Form as she cuddled her eggs unseen in bowers
beneath grass shadows just
Like the stripes on her feathers; tiny
hummingbird's handy gadget for

Tapping the sweetness in flowers; and
Mother Monarch Butterfly's odd
Featherbed she made for her babes
in the milkweed pod.
She had us taste musky morels, sugar plum sweet,
wild raspberry parfait, gooseberry treat,
Wintergreen berries, mint from the spring,
bitter acorn, pepperroot sting.
No sense she neglected. We learned, detected the
difference in feel, the prickle and
Tickle as it were of fur; rough hazelnut "burr",
soft pussytoes, velvet mullen,

The Farm

Sharp needles of spruce. Smells of
Balm of Gilead, wild cherry, Labrador tea,
She whetted our appetites for pleasures
of sight. We were wakened at night
To delight in the fiery flaring
borealis, and the twin lights that were
Roebucks eyes as he stood
browsing our garden greens. Late
Evenings she showed us where the
rotting wood in phosphorescence glowed,
Moon's shimmering face reflected where
quiet water blackly flowed.

In spring she knew where violets first
burst into view, anemones blew,
The dainty Maiden Hair unfurled,
and woodfern curled its dainty green
Fronds. As the season advanced we
chanced upon the ghostly Indian pipe;
Cranberries as they trailed in cranberry bogs
their red lacy vines, and the bramble
Where honeysuckle twines; there we scrambled through
to Wren's dainty nest,
She waded up to her knees in gup that she might float
one delicate waterlily in a cup.

I see her still as she stood on the
crest of the hill, tiny of stature
But tall of will; white curls awry
against the blue sky; striped

Floursackapron picking up the yelloworangegreen of
overgrownacres rank with
Hawkweed. Not all the priests in all the
churches in all the Land can
Speak so clearly, "The Purpose and Plan"
as this one small person;
God's flower in hand, her rich soul
loving, "The Jack in the Pulpit."

Grandma [Martha Jones Halstead] was also very adventurous. Uncle James was the only bachelor in the family. He was 4 or 5 years older than mother but to me he always looked old as he had a shy shuffling gait, and was slightly hunched over. He smoked a pipe at times and cigarettes at other times. Whether it was his bachelor status or his smoking or just plain a lack of bathing, he seemed to have a 'needing a shave' look. You never got the feeling that he had just stepped out of the shower!! Anyway, Uncle James worked at odd jobs, some construction, handyman and farmland types but mostly construction. He almost always lived with Grandma. Eighty acres of the farm was Uncle James', and Bob says he had a home on that 80 acres too. I don't remember that but Bob was 10

James *(l)* and Tom *(r)*.

years older than I. It was inevitable, when James went West to work on the many Federal Dam Projects in the late 40's and 50's, that Grandma went with him.

> *Jim* [Myrtle's son]: Uncle James always did this little Russian dance. He played the harmonica and the squeeze box.. After Grandma died in 1958, he did a lot of travelling around and spent some time at some hot springs in Arkansas. In the 70's he went and lived with those people in Chatham. Evidently he'd get his check and pay them and then he could spend the rest. He ate with them so he always had something to eat.

I know I've jumped around some here but hopefully I'll fill in the spaces as I go. I was telling about Grandma and got sidetracked to Uncle James; but he did play a big part in Grandma's life, which was all a part of Alice.

Back to the early life of Alice. The farm had chickens, a big garden and at least one cow, so there were many chores to keep the whole family busy. The garden was big in potatoes, rutabagas, squash, beans, peas, carrots and things they could either store (in the root cellar) or can. So between cultivating with horse and plow in the spring, and the final harvest in the fall, there was plenty to do. Daily the chickens needed to be fed, the eggs collected, the cow milked, the garden cultivated, and/or planted or picked. When the milk supply exceeded demand, there was butter to be made and fresh buttermilk to go with the fragrant bread right out of the oven. So everyone took part in the chores and watching the younger children.

> *Bob*: One time Grandma was out cleaning the barn. Old Barney was one of the horses … Old Barney and King. Barney was really a gentle, gentle horse, and what happened is, when Grandma was cleaning out the stall, she accidently poked Old Barney down in the foot area, and he kicked her. He was a mellow horse but when she picked him with that pitchfork, he kicked and it broke her leg. Then she spent quite a bit of time at our house, as she was quite old then, you know, (about 60, I think). That was when we lived at Rock. She'd take a bath

every day and the leg healed up. They didn't think she'd ever walk again, but she became just as spry as could be.

Janis: You've probably heard the story of when Grandma's leg was broken. You weren't born yet and I was only 3 or 4. Grandma was doing something with the horses in the barn, and one of the horses kicked her accidently and broke her leg. She couldn't walk and so she lay there for a number of hours before Uncle James found her. So they took her to the hospital. In those days they took you to the hospital if anything happened to you. So they cast her leg and brought her home to our house. They put her up in what was then my room, the green room, to recuperate. The word was that Grandpa was going to bother her and she was supposed to have peace and quiet. Nobody was supposed to tell Grandpa where she was. So I had been instructed not to tell Grandpa where she was. I was sitting on the front porch when he came up to the steps. I knew even as young as I was that he had to travel a number of miles in the old car to see Grandma. He was all dressed up like he dressed, and he said, "Where's Martha?" I just remember the terrible feeling I had about him wanting to see Grandma and I, even as small as I was, felt it was his right even though I wasn't supposed to tell him. I was tongue-tied and then he said, "Well, I know they've got her hidden here but I just want to see how she is." He just walked away. I guess he was scared of my mother which I could understand 'cause at that age I was afraid of her too!!!!!

Uncle Tom was the oldest boy, and in the early 1900's if a family was not well to do, the older children at 13 went out on their own. I don't know what Uncle Tom went out to do, but I'll ask his daughter Gladys and fill in the details later. The important thing is that all these kids really knew how to work and from their steady guidance from Grandma and strong value on education, 4 out of 8 children got college degrees. The ones who didn't get degrees achieved also,

Uncle Tom-*b. 1898*

but achieved on their own. Imagine, after leaving home at 13, Alice put herself through high school, and then through two years of college which at that time was a teaching degree.

I just made arrangements to spend some time with Joan [Gladys' daughter] Tom's granddaughter. I'll see what I can learn about Uncle Tom.

Jim: Tom was my mother's oldest brother. My mom [Myrtle] was the oldest. Tom only went through the 4th grade, but he was intelligent enough to be workin' on the atomic bomb during World War II. He was getting a thousand dollars a month pay at that time because of his expertise. The government was actually paying him, it was a cost plus type thing. This is what my mother told me.

Joan [Tom's granddaughter]: I can remember I got a lot of what I know from Alice's stories about the family. I got a sense that the family growing up was not so much of a family because the older ones were leaving before the younger ones were born. Tom had left before Clara, Charlie and Jack were born. What she did tell me was that Tom left home at maybe 11 or 12, to be assistant to a cook helper in the lumber camps.. I'm not sure how often he got home but he was on his own supporting himself from that early age. That seemed to temper his entire life…, his independence and his attitude toward his own children and grandchildren. You make it on your own—it'll make you a better person. We didn't want to hear that when we grandchildren were struggling, holding down three jobs trying to get through college. [Tom had two children, Evelyn, and Gladys, Joan's mom.] He had all this money and he'd say, "I lost $10,000 on the stock market today," and not blink an eye and here were all these grandchildren without a penny. He was adamant about wanting them to make it on their own and earn their way through.

It was my impression that after the lumber camps, he'd gone down to Detroit. While he was employed he went to night school and picked up his degrees or accounting ability, whatever he had, that way. He found his niche with the company. I believe he worked for Dodge in accounting, having to do with payroll. He had a real knack for doing this estimating of money paid to payroll, so that when he finally had to retire, it took several people to replace him. Even during the Depression he was always employed, he was so valuable. My mom's recollections—she saw others picking through the trash cans and the poverty all around but she never wanted for anything during the Depression. I don't think she had the effects of a lot of people who went through the Depression that lasted their whole lives. You know the type that washed ice cubes and reused them and hanging up paper towels to dry and reusing them.

Myrtle was the oldest of the family. Mother's older sister. I never saw too much of Myrtle as by the time I was old enough to remember, she moved her family out to Oregon.

Aunt Myrtle-*b. 1896*

Bob: When Mom [Myrtle] was 13 or 14, she went working some place. She used to tell me that she gave quite a percentage of her salary back to her parents, because they were pretty hard up, you know. I don't know where she went working. Later on she went to college to become a teacher. She did that before they got married. She taught school for a little while and they got married. Then she never taught school again until after my dad passed away.

Jim: She [Myrtle] lived in Wisconsin, did housework and went to school. She went all the way through 2 years of college, Normal School. After that, she met Dad, and she never did teach after that. She was coming home on the train when she met my Dad.

James was next in line. I've already told a little about him, the family bachelor. Another story I heard about him was that he was drafted into the service during World War II and he was already 40 or so. He was discharged in 1945 in Texas and so he decided to see the country before he came home. He really liked travelling.

This would be Alice's place in the family. She was born in 1909.

George was between Alice and Clara. Boy, did Clara ever adore her big brother George.

Loraine [George's wife]: When George left home at 13 it was to work on a farm in Indiana. From there he moved on to road construction and the building of the Pennsylvania turnpike. I guess he was a shovel operator for that job. After the war, when he moved to Detroit, he first worked as a Radial Drill Press Operator. Then he worked with Uncle Tom where he was an Excavation Engineer.

Uncle George-*b.1911*

During World War II, George was a Sea Bee. A black and gold bee was the logo for the Construction Battalion and I believe he was somewhere in England. I remember really liking his 'patch' on his Navy uniform.

I remember that patch but I didn't discover what the Sea Bees were until I was much older. I was only between 3 and 7 during the war. I also have a picture of him in a kilt in Scotland. I remember he was in the Navy and looked particularly handsome in his uniform. He learned construction in the Navy.

Sally, Sport, Grandma at Fox farm in 1940s.

After marrying Loraine he came up to Escanaba area (the farm at Fox) and turned Grandma's farm there (he had bought it from Uncle James) into a beautiful lakeside motel and resort. Starting work on this before Loraine came up to live, she would joke, "Save some work for me." Famous last words. Part of the old farmhouse became a restaurant and George, Loraine, and Marilyn, their daughter, lived there and ran the whole operation. I was particularly fond of Uncle George.

Clara is next down the line. I have letters of her high school years which I will get to later.

Charlie was the seventh living child. There were two other children born who didn't make it. One was Robert who died at birth. The other was Sarah who died of mastitis at about age two. I guess two out of ten is not too bad in those days. All children were born at home except the last one, Jack.

Jackie: [Charlies wife]: Charlie left home when he was fourteen. He went to high school in Munising. He stayed with Clara and Ole for four years. He graduated from Mather in 1938 and he got all honors and a scholarship to Michigan Tech at Houghton. So he went to see about going there. What the scholarship paid was the tuition, but he'd have to pay for his books and his boarding and all that. Since there was no money, he decided to go down to Detroit and live with Tom and Mary. He thought maybe he could get a job and work for a year but there were no jobs around. So he joined the Army Air Corps. Well, in the meantime the war came along and he was in for six years.

Charlie came home on a visit from the service and Gladys [Tom and Mary's daughter] kept saying to me, "You should marry one of my uncles." I went to college with Gladys and that was the big joke. We did meet and he came over to see me after he came back from the service. He just said he was going to go up to school, as he was all registered. He said, "Are you interested?" I said, "I don't know." I didn't really know him. So he stayed down there and he got a job and he worked for a while so we could go out and get acquainted. It worked out that I did fall in love with him and we got engaged at Christmas time which was very neat. We got married and I stayed down here for the rest of the term. Then I moved up there with him for the rest of his schooling [Mechanical Engineering] which was paid by the G.I. Bill.

(l-r): Grandpa, Jack, Charley, and Alice.

Uncle Jack, often called John, was the youngest in the family. Madelyn, Jack's wife, was unable to give me information but Janis was able to fill me in on a few details of his life. I guess there was a high school in that area by that time and so he went to it. We think it was in Trenary. In the winter he stayed with the Andersons on the main road and he and the Anderson boy his age took the bus together. Janis remembers when one of the sisters, Myrtle, Alice or Clara, asked how Jack was doing in school and Grandma said, "Not too well—he got all D's." So he joined the Navy in 1942. He was only 17, so the story goes that he lied about his age to get in. He had a jaunty air about him and loved to joke. As he was younger than the other uncles, I felt a kinship, being the youngest myself. He served in the Pacific and when he got out, he went to Michigan Tech on the G.I. Bill. His degree was in Civil Engineering and his first job in '48 was building a road in Brazil.

> *Jim*: When I was 16 in 1952, Grandma was living with John [Uncle Jack must have been back from Brazil] and Jim [Uncle James] and me, and we travelled all over the place. We travelled from construction site to construction site and I'd always get a job. Every place we'd stop we'd work.
>
> John was working with us and he wrecked his Kaiser car, totalling it out, a '51 Kaiser, the one he got when he got out of school. It was really funny. First of all James got in a little wreck ... I take that back, I was the first one to wreck my car. Then James got into a little fender bender, then John wrecks his car. Within a month all three of us wrecked our cars. Jame's pickup wasn't hurt very bad, only $50.00 to fix it. But John's car and my car were both totalled. Grandma and James stayed up in Irrigon, Oregon, where they were renting this little cabin. So my mother [Mother's older sister], my sister MaryJane, and brother Pat came and we were all living in this little cabin. The insurance company sent back our premiums, no more insurance. Uncle Jim got a double fracture of the skull at the bridge of his nose. John was by himself and he rolled his down into the Umatilla River, that's in Oregon.
>
> We lived in Irrigon, Oregon [no longer an incorporated town] at that time, and we worked on that dam, all three of us. So then we got laid off at the dam, so we loaded up and we trav-

elled around. We went to Sacramento first,...four of us in that pick-up at this time was pretty damn crowded. So from Sacramento we went out and bought some lumber and we built a canopy for the pick-up, so one of us could ride in the back. Grandma, she liked it back there the best, so she rode there the most. We all smoked, puffin' away all the time, so I imagine Grandma, as she had a cough, liked to get away from the smoke. I remember some little town we stopped in they had free chest x-rays so we said, "Grandma, we're going to go get your chest x-rayed to make sure there's nothin' the matter with you with that cough you've got all the time." So we went to Arizona, Nevada, and California. I got a job at the city of San Francisco, and John, he got a job in Alaska. So he left right then, and left us right on the spot. James and Ma and I lived in another two room cabin kinda with an outhouse, a three-holer outhouse, and it had running cold water, a wood stove and a hot plate. Had to go next door to get a shower, to get cleaned up.

After this I believe Jack met Madeline and they went back to South America. Maybe Venezuela this time. It didn't work out for them so they came back to California. Then Jack got a job with the State and eventually became the Northern California Chief Dam Inspector.

Anyway, let's go back to the farm and find out about Grandpa Halstead.

Bob: Grandpa and Grandma homesteaded 80 acres of land up there at Limestone and so did Uncle James. 80 acres connecting to their 80. What they did with this property was ... they used to make railroad ties. They'd cut down trees and then cut the logs up in lengths for a tie and hand hew those things for the railroad company. They had to work someplace and the only job they could get at that time was what they could use off of that land. That was a good thing 'cause there was a lot of timber on that land and they both worked making railroad

Grandpa in Munising.

ties. Also they both had to improve the property. [Homestead Law required building on the property.] They made ties for the [rail] turns because they were worth more money. They were made out of hardwood, and the railroad used those on turns where they'd get more stress. So that's the kind they made. So Uncle James never left home like the other kids. He did have a home on his 80 acres too.

Janis: I've got a couple of memories of Grandpa and I'm not even sure which one comes first 'cause I was very small. I was only 4 when he died. The one memory I have is of being out to Grandma's farm, you know in that old house, sitting on Grandpa's knee. He's holding me on his lap, and the dog came in. Now the door was this old fashioned Upper Michigan door kind of thing. I mean not only did it not have a knob and a latch but the door stayed closed because one piece of wood stuck out and as it closed over another piece of wood it kind of held the door closed. There was a way you could draw a piece of wood over it to bolt it ... as I recall. Anyway, the dog came in as the door opened inward, so the dog just had to push the door to open it. So, the dog came in and I was sitting on Grandpa's lap and he said "Okay, Rover (not sure of his name) were you born in a barn? Close the door!!!!!." And the dog raised

Grandma and Grandpa's wedding

up on his hind legs and pushed the door closed. So I have that nice memory of Grandpa. Now, he wasn't a very tall man. I have a nice picture of him. Do you have it? Grandma was only 4 ft. 11 in. or so and he wasn't very tall either, maybe 5 ft. 1 or 2 in. Very small people in those days. You know he was mostly Irish, as far as I know.

Bob: I used to gather eggs for Grandma. She'd send me out to give me somethin' to do, so I'd go out to the henhouse and gather the eggs. This one day, I had come back with those eggs, you know, and Grandpa happened to be sittin' outside after he came back from where he'd been workin' in the woods. He called me over so I went over and sat by him for a while. Then he picked up one of them eggs and he poked the teeniest little hole in that egg you ever did see with his knife, and he took and he sucked that raw egg out of that teeny little hole, and he took and he put that egg back in amongst the other eggs, and he told me, "Now, don't tell Grandma what I did now!!".

My mother always told me that if it wasn't for the booze, he'd a become a real famous person 'cause he was so intelligent. He mostly drank his moonshine … on a weekend. 'Course that's when we'd all go visit!!! So where we'd see him would be out in a kinda like a lean-to shed he had there. That was where he slept 'cause there was too much noise in the house. All the kids would be there on a Sunday. We'd all see each other there at the old farm at Limestone. Charlie was kind of moving out about that time, but Jack was still there. It was about the same time that Dorothy [Bob's sister] was getting out on her own. Fact is, she worked near there, Chatham I think. She worked for somebody that rented rooms and she used to take in wash, and iron clothes for the renters of these rooms. She'd steam press with a mangle. Then the next job she had was pretty much up around that way too, when she started waiting tables. That was about the time we moved up to Sands. Then we moved here [in St. Ignace] and she met Bob Gilly. Then her and Bob Gilly got married. Gert [another sister] also got married in St Ignace, to Andy.

The barn was out in back. The other shed might have been where they lived before they built the log home. After the old barn got too dilapidated...or did it burn down when James fell asleep with a cigarette...they used the other outbuilding for a barn.

Gladys: Grandpa was the one that did all the talking about the politics. He was handsome and had some curls too. We went once to the Jones's [Grandma's maiden name was Jones] at Cornucopia—[Wisconsin]—they were having a big reunion and I met lots of cousins—and we went out fishing.

Janis: Mother always talked about how her parents helped her with her math. Grandpa would just look at the problem and knew the answer but he didn't know how he got the answer. Then Grandma would figure out how you got to the answer. One time the answer in the back of the book was different than the one he came up with so he wrote to the textbook company. They were wrong. We're talking about 4th grade math here.

Grandpa was on the School Board in Limestone. He had fought the School Board, you see, because they wouldn't provide transportation for his kids. He kept them out of school for a whole year in protest. They had to walk 3 miles. I suppose he fought with the Road Commission too about the roads. His family's background was in mathematics.. I guess some of his uncles or someone in his family discovered some mathematic formula. He was a professor or something. There was a lot of that type of brains on that side of the family.

I know Grandma's forebears came from Door County—Fish Creek—do you know where Grandpa's came from? How did they meet?

Janis: My speculation is—because of them having relatives in Appleton, Wisconsin, and Fish Creek being on the Door Peninsula, they were in the same area. Great Aunt Alice, Grandpa's sister, that mother was named after, she taught piano down there. Mother was always fond of her. My speculation is they met somewhere there, because they ran away together when they were 17. Grandpa worked as a lumberjack then. I know they moved many, many times from lumber camp to lumber camp...because Aunt Clara told me when she was moving from her old rental house to the house they built first, she had written to her mother telling about all this stuff she had and how hard it was to move. It must have sounded like a complaining letter to Grandma, 'cause she wrote back. That letter was read to me about all the places Grandma had moved. Those letters might be in the old garage down at Clara's as John said he moved that stuff from the house to the garage.

Grandma and Grandpa homesteaded that place in Limestone we remember after mother was born, because she tells a story about when they moved to one of those numerous places, she found, in the chink in the logs, this little tiny doll. It was the only doll she ever had!!! Then when they settled there in Limestone, Aunt Clara tells about picking rocks and picking rocks and picking rocks out of the fields.

One story about Grandpa was that he could dance an Irish Jig. And another one was that he talked with people after they died. He believed that people came and visited him after they died. The bad stories I just heard bits of too. He was angry once, he'd probably come home drunk, anyway, he was chasing Grandma with an ax, and she took the kids and went and hid in the loft of someone else's barn. They didn't like to talk about this stuff.

About Grandpa's death ... I got this from Mother's recall when I was working with her after I became a psychologist. The horse and wagon got stuck in the river, and Grandpa got real wet and couldn't get them out. Uncle James found him the next morning and he was still alive and said "Tell them all I love them."

When I asked others what they knew about Grandpa's death, I got a variety of stories. All in all it was memorable.

Aunt Jackie: Grandpa Halstead died in the wintertime. He and James were walking to town. [Limestone?] It was very cold and they were walking along and he dropped dead. So they brought the body in and they put it on the bed. James said he'd go into town to get the undertaker. So he went to Munising and there was a tremendous storm and he couldn't get back. So there poor Grandma sat with the body in that little cabin. He couldn't get back for two days so she had to just wait. I guess he died of a heart attack.

Bob: In the spring of the year it used to flood a lot up there at Rock where we lived and also around Limestone. During this time of the year, Uncle James and Grandpa walked into town to get some groceries and on the way back from town, they got to a kind of high spot that wasn't so wet, and Grandpa wanted to sit down. That's when he passed away.

Mother's poem about Grandpa written in the 60's says alot.

HE,

Our Dear Papa, DEAD DRUNK, with whiskey he stunk; but,
Who shall put him into a mold?
An embodiment of contrasts, tender musings, loud bombasts,
the sparkle, drama of our lives,
The witty, the whimsical, capricious, shy, changeable,
freakish, fanciful, chimerical,
Crotchety, kind, cozily tender and sweet. A sad
excuse of a man, wasted, degenerate,
Slipping downgrade. Sturdy, strong, turning weak,
ill, complaining, chaining himself to his bed.
Then up at early April's dawn to till, to build the soil,
to spread with his hand the seed of clover,
Timothy, grain,. Later as it leaned green in the wind
we admired with him its beauty.

Who shall know him?

Born and bred of a family of worth, spent his
Irish wit in mirth born of tragedy.
His expression of Art aborted when his father snorted,
"There will be no sissies in this family."
His advanced soul distorted, he resorted to living
thirstily. His fine mind untrained
He early left the hearth, making lumbermans's tracks
over much of the U.P. With his axe-edged keen
He led the crew from dawn to dark, driving the team,
swinging the beam, peeling the bark,
Riding the ark of logs downstream. He drowned his
aspirations in monthly celebrations, taking
Swigs of whiskey straight from the jug.

Who shall understand him?

Reckless, strong, weak, pushed from the nest before he
could fly. Dejected; rejected by his mother,
"You must impress the neighbors;" he felt compelled to rebel
against society. He loved his wife with her
Strength stressed his weakness. He loved his children
who with their success underlined his failure.
His first kiss with whiskey excused him from remission
of expression. Beneath his clowning was his
Drowning, his groping grasping for the real. He became
a sport, the likeable sort, dancing, singing,
Jigging, entertaining with his heel. Tales he would spiel so real
we never knew if they were fact or fiction.

Who shall love him?

His tenderness, his gaiety, his warmth, his love
of humanity, his stillness for life,
His kind generosity, his meaning to be good, his ambition
too high to reach, his qualms, his misgivings,
His ever resolve to outdo himself, his self-unforgiveness,
his winning ways with people, his friendliness?

Who shall see him?

His Joy, his sinking to the depths, his within struggle
to rise to the surface, his spurious instancy
Always striving with his desire for attainment, his love
of truth, his perceptive beauty of the newborn, his
Insight into the growing child, his quick and accurate reasoning,
his reading to seek, to find, the Without within?

Who shall honor him?

Tom? "he was sensitive to himself, a fool to others."
Myrtle? "I pray for his soul."
James? "He both protected me and rejected me, and said
at his death, 'Tell them I loved them all.' "
Alice? "I love him; but love's indecision turned to derision,
then later (the fashion) became compassion."
George? "His is the Song of the Barroom Floor."
Charles? (Whipped, beaten, coddled, spoiled at his caprice,)
"I admired his mind, grieved for his demise."
John? "His drinking rolled off me as raindrops from a
duck's back."
His friends? "We were sorry for his family, but found him
a friend among friends, a neighbor among neighbors."

Who shall judge him?

Himself? "Why am I here? I'd like to find out.
Where do I start? Would I find the true me in the
Expression of art? I made a wrong turning, with whiskey
I'm burning. I am bound. I have found no way
Through the maze. I love my children who think I am rot,
I love my wife, without her I'm not;
Though I spout figures to confound professors,
I must confess I'm a genius turned inside out.
I love politics, I'm at home in this field, great charm
I wield. With an education I'd have gone to the top,
Without one, I'll have to stop here in the Township. I'll drink
myself to death, shine as host at my own funeral."

Who shall mourn him?

His wife "He tries. He fails. It is discouraging for him
to live with himself. For me
It is hell to live with him. The children
are fortunate. They see,
They learn, they leave. I have lost hope.
I will stand by till his death, then live free.
I support him in good, ignore him in bad.
He is a good man, undone."

Who shall justify?

His minister? "I thought him to be the greatest man
I ever buried. The whole county
Turned out to praise him. I place his name 'in the book of gold,'
as one who loved his fellowmen."

Who shall praise him?

His children? For the fine brains he bestowed through
his genes, their inheritance? His openness
For Truth? His voracity for learning? His taking over
the administration that we might all have an
Education? His inebriety, that we all chose sobriety?
A cemented loyalty, one for the other, each for
Father, Mother? The color, light, spontaneity his
Irish wit gave us? Real Love?
Responsiveness to people? For the glorious
days we spent in his company,
Beside him, thistles whistling to his scythe?
circling birds' nests in the grass as we passed?

Wetting and turning the stone as he honed his axe?
Visiting with him each Roundup, Picnic, Fair.
Sitting beside him on the seat of the wagon
or tucked in the lap on the way
To a Christmas Play, the harness jingling
our song of happiness. Or,
Munching the treats he brought us to eat,
squashed penny chocolates in his pockets,
The grouse he shot one the wing, speckled trout,
first catch of spring, or,
Bonbons to save and to savor as we might well
the flavor of his life.

Who shall say?

But that each of us found our degree of success
in the strange arrangement of
Peace and duress that blessed our growing up;
and that his life was well spent,
Lent itself to expansion, and his soul has now
found its new mansion?

Who shall tell him?

All is well with us

Katie Reffruschinni

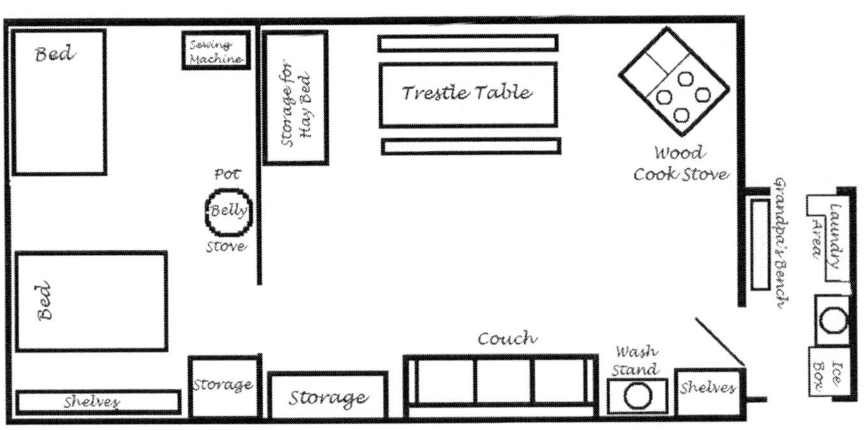

Munising

GETTING BACK TO THE 1920'S, Alice also left home at 13 or 14. Or so I've been told. That would have been 1922 or 23. I don't have any exact sequence of events in her home life during that time, but I do have a lot of fragments of her stories from that era of her life.

> *Janis*: This may not be accurate but these are the pictures in my head when mother told me this story. It was time for the Alger County Fair and I don't remember where it was, maybe Chatham, or maybe Munising. So Grandpa was going to take mother this one year to the fair. She was about 13 and through grammar school and it was time for her to find a place to stay so she could go to high school in Munising. It was a special trip for her 'cause she didn't very often get to go, just her and her father. When she told me, I pictured them going with horse and buggy and I pictured it in Munising. By horse and buggy that would have been a two hour trip each way. When they got there, he talked to a lot of people to find out who might need someone to help in the house. Someone who might be willing to provide room and board for the household help. This was after Emeline Tredway had her stroke. They had a full time housekeeper but in those days people had servants. When they had money, instead of buying a boat they bought a maid!! I think Emeline was ill at the time because they had a housekeeper, but the housekeeper thought she needed help. So it was at this fair, by talking around to different buddies and people he knew, that grandpa found that Mr. Tredway was looking for somebody. To mother it was a magic day—sort of like it was meant to be.

So, to my knowledge, that was what she did. She lived with the Tredways, Owen and Emeline, and did housework in return for room and board. Now the Tredways hadn't had any children and at this time, Owen would have been around 57 or 58. His wife was ailing and needed help. So Alice became like a daughter to them.

> *Janis*: Daddy came from the working class. His father was a carpenter, a builder. Daddy started out as a salesman, you know, of drugs (pharmaceuticals), and saved his money. That's how he got ahead. He got a Pharmacist Degree and got a job for a drug company. You know how you go around and talk to the doctors and drug stores and get their accounts. That's what he did. Then he travelled through the U.P. and eventually got a job up in Marquette as a pharmacist in a drug store.

So Owen met Emeline in Marquette and he decided to settle there. It was 1896 that he set out on his own in Munising. It was just beginning to be settled. So he became a pioneer in Munising and built Tredway's Drug Store with an apartment over it. That's where he and Emeline lived then, until he built the house on Chocolay Street in 1919.

Owen had one sister, Ella Stinson, who had one daughter, Marie, who was married to John Haglund. Marie was older than mother was and also like a daughter to the Tredways. Marie had four children, Tredway (who I interviewed), Ann, Dick, and Barbara.

> *Tredway:* I heard the story many times how Grandma [Ella] couldn't take care of Mom [Marie]. So when Mom was twelve or thirteen, she went up to Munising and did the rest of her school up there. Uncle Owen was her father from that time on, I guess. She stayed right there with Emeline and Uncle Owen just like their own child you see. Then she went away to Normal School and after she graduated, she went to Gwinn to teach. She was probably about 20. She met my dad and they got married and we lived over there in Gwinn for about a year or so. Dad was a chemist working for the iron mines [Cleveland Cliffs Iron Co] and he probably lost his job there so we went to Munising. Apparently, we stayed above the store there in that apartment. He got a job with Thor Holter as a plumber's apprentice and learned the plumbing trade. All of us kids were two years apart. I was born in 1921. Ann and Dick came next, and then we went to Casnovia for that year Barbara (Bing) was born.

Now I'm pretty sure that when mother worked for Marie she was quite young, and was going to high school. She was helping Marie out with Tredway and maybe Ann, Marie's oldest two kids. She was also doing some housework for some pin money. It's my understanding that Marie at this time lived in an apartment over Tredway's Drug Store in Munising, which is the big town mother travelled to in order to go to high school in 1923 or so. Later you will see there was some competitive feelings between Marie and my Mom.

> *Tredway*: I remember Alice working for my mother. I heard someone say you could touch a hot stove, but she told me not to. I guess I did anyway, and I got burnt. I got along good with Alice. She knew me best. She used to read me stories at bedtime. But for the life of me I can't remember if she stayed at our house and slept there 'cause there wasn't much room there above the store. I know I went to Kindergarten there at the school across the street from Uncle Owen's house, but I don't remember going back and forth to school at all. I have a picture of me, Bob Holter, and Bill Bauman out in the snow in front of the store there and I vaguely remember playing with those guys. We lived there over the store in downtown Munising, 1925-26, the Tredway Drug Store.

An article from an Alger County Heritage Newsletter may give you a little more history of Owen, his store, and his earlier life.

FOLKS REMEMBERED

by Faye Swanberg

Owen R. Tredway was one of the first businessmen to settle in Munising. A depression was in progress in 1896 when the young pharmacist moved his wife from Marquette to the raw settlement springing up in a cedar swamp on the shore of Munising Bay. Just three women had braved the rigors of the wilderness to accompany their husbands before Mrs. Tredway arrived.

O.R. Tredway was born in Casnovia, near Grand Rapids, on September 6, 1864. Upon completing school at age 15, he worked with his father, who was the village carpenter. His spare time was

Owen and Emeline Tredway, dressed in the ski costumes of the day, are probably heading for one of the outings of the Viking Ski Club. Organized by the Norwegians who introduced skiing - especially ski jumping to Munising in 1905, the club's activities centered around their clubhouse on the Munising Papermill property. The regular ski treks were well attended at a time when residents made their own fun, and the sociable Tredways were part of them.

spent hanging around the local drug store, which led finally in 1885 to his enrollment in a 2-year course at the Chicago School of Pharmacy. He then followed his profession successively in Coopersville, Michigan, Detroit, in 10 states as traveling salesman, Chicago and lastly in Pendill's Pharmacy in Marquette. It was in Marquette that he married Emeline VanWyck of Otsego, Michigan, on February 20, 1888.

A popular form of recreation at the time was boat excursions to picturesque sites along Lake Superior. Around 1891, the Tredways with others hired a tug for a memorable trip to Pictured Rocks. When a few years later Owen heard of the new town starting in the area, he knew that here, finally, was the place to launch his own business.

On New Years Day in 1896, Tredway took the train to Wetmore from where local dreyman, George O'Donnel, tucked him into his horse drawn sleigh to deliver him to the site he was to call home for the rest of his life. A handful of buildings quickly constructed the previous fall had broken a townsite still more virgin forest than settlement. Trails wandered amongst fresh stumps westward in the direction of sawmills being built on the lakeshore. From the almost unlimited choices, Tredway selected a lot in the 200 block of W. Superior Street, just east of the present Tourville building.

In April, he returned with his father who had come from Lower Michigan to assist him in building his store. After scratching around in the snow to locate a lot cornerpost, they proceeded to put up a shack on the back of the lot in which the three Tredways would live until the store was completed, when they moved into the upstairs apartment. With the spring thaw came the realization that the drainage from the hill back of the townsite made theirs and many others a rather soggy site. Nevertheless, they proceeded and with $500 to invest in stock and equipment, the determined Tredway opened one of the earliest businesses in Munising.

Tredway's Drug on a wintry day in downtown Munising

A year or so later, he moved his store intact to its present site, the home of Lester's Jewelry. [Where Lester's was in the 1980's. Now I believe its a Dentists Office]. The operation took a week. As yet there were no office buildings so Dr. Grawn, an early practitioner, opened for business in the rear of Tredway's store.

The enterprising Tredway also took over the management of Sam Meyer's Opera House. [In the 40's and 50's this was Burn's Department Store until it became People's Store. Now it is divided into several small businesses.] At the time, it was the only place in town for road shows, dances, lectures, caucuses basketball, suppers and wrestling matches. It was the last place of worship for Methodists before construction of the church in 1897. When Meyers left town, Tredway bought the lucrative business and operated it until the Delft Theater was constructed in 1915.

With an architect, Tredway planned the family home at 115 E. Chocolay Street and again called on the expertise of his father to build it. It remained the family home until the death of the second Mrs. Tredway in 1987.

Owen in early 1900s

A young Norwegian, Oscar Oie, came from Ishpeming in 1903 to work for Tredway, January 1 was becoming a significant date for the gentle druggist. On January 1, 1920, he took Oie in as a quarter partner. He remarried in 1932, to Alice Halstead, and to the couple were born two girls, Janis and Palma. On January 1, 1947, he sold his share of the business to Oie, but continued to fill in at the store. Just a year later, Owen R. Tredway died.

The mild mannered pharmacist was community minded. Among

the offices he held were Munising Township Treasurer and Trustee on the Board of Education. He played a leading role in the Methodist Episcopal Church and was a member of the Masonic Lodge and the Shrine. Tredway was an early promoter of skiing in Munising but it was golfing that he ardently pursued over the years.

Although it has been 41 years since the white-maned Tredway has been seen on his daily walks to this store, the pioneering druggist in the store with the pull down cigar lighter remains a delightful memory for many of us.

When Alice arrived in Munising, the house at 115 Chocolay Street had been recently constructed, designed and built by Owen and his father Benjamin Stacey.

It was located across the street from Mather School where students went to school from kindergarten to twelfth grade. The house faces south with a large brown brick front porch. It was a great porch because on cold, summer, north wind days, we could sit on the sun warmed concrete steps and be sheltered from the wind. On the other hand, hot, muggy, south wind days, we could sit on the wicker porch swing and catch any small puff of wind. Though this was Chocolay Street, not Maple Street, there were big Norway maples making the street shaded and cozy.

The front door was a heavy oak door with 12 beveled glass panes. Upon entering that door we were in a vestibule that had a bench for taking off boots, coat hooks, and a closet with a full length mirror. The floor was a brown and white ceramic mosaic tile. Now, we entered the house through another wood door, this one birch, which also had 12 panes of beveled glass!!! This house is important to this story as it was a very big part of Alice's life. She was proud, attached, and very protective of it.

Inside the second front door, slightly to the right was the staircase going upstairs. To the left was the living room, and above was a beautiful brass chandelier, and finished birch beams. The fireplace was of a brown brick which matched the brick on the porch and had a finished birch mantel. It faced the door and the couch which was on the

Alice in her teens

front wall of the house. At the far end of the room was a bay window area which faced the street. Below the windows was a low, wide, radiator with a board with a padded cover on it. I remember many times coming in from outside with numb feet and fingers, sitting there to warm up, my feet burning and prickling as they lost their numbness!!! The upper half of the double hung windows were divided into small panes as were all the windows in the house.

Can you imagine a fourteen year old Alice walking in this house to live and go to school after coming from that two-room log cabin in Limestone?

The piano, in the early years of my life, was in the corner below the stairs. While it was there it was a great place for hiding behind as it was kiddie corner across the bannister to the stairs and we could swing down behind it from the bannister!!!! In later years it was moved to the far end of the living room against the west wall. The piano itself had its own story. It was built in the 1890's and had been used in the Opera House in downtown Munising during the years of the follies. The ornate case was black and somewhat battered but still was beautiful, especially to me who loved the piano and its music as long as I can remember. I remember Mother telling me, "I'll do the dishes while you practice your lesson." She didn't want us to hate doing the dishes so I very seldom had to do them. I don't mind doing the dishes to this day.

The dining room and kitchen were behind the living room, stairs area. Coming into the dining room from the far end of the living room were built in bookcases that were below lovely birch finished pillars. The bookcases had leaded glass doors that were fragile. The dining room had wainscotting and a built-in buffet, with a mirror between the cabinets, which also had leaded glass doors. There were windows with many small panes on the west side of the room. The center of the room held a heavy round oak table and chairs with a chandelier over it which had a white, figured glass globe, identical in shape to the two with brass globes in the living room.

Going on into the kitchen through a swinging door, straight ahead was a pastry cabinet which had a cutting board surface and tin flour bins and another cutting, pastry board that pulled out from it. I remember "helping'" mother make cinnamon rolls on that board one time before I could read. All the spices cans looked alike because we got them from the Co-op where we shopped. I spread the butter on the rolled out dough, packed on the brown sugar using lots so they'd be real gooey and then sprinkled on the "cinnamon" real thick. I think I started sneezing then and Mother came in and shrieked, as the can of "cinnamon" was really black pepper!!! We scraped it off and salvaged the rolls, but boy, I never helped out again for a while without mother's close supervision.

On the right was an early 20's electric stove that had long legs. Just to the left in a pantry was a General Electric refrigerator that had the motor on the top. You can imagine my dismay as a 50's teenager having these antiquated appliances at my house. But to Alice in the early twenties these appliances probably were amazing, after the old wood stove and icebox at home. The sink looked out on the back porch, garage, and back yard.

Completing the circle downstairs, because it was a circle that we as kids used to run round and round, was a small hallway with hooks where we hung our coats, and the door to the basement. The first thing you saw in the basement was a 'cold' room for storing vegetables and canned goods, a wringer washer, and a small wood stove for heating wash water. The big coal furnace with an automatic hopper took up the center of that space, with a room called the coal bin from which we filled the hopper. The coal truck would back into the driveway, put down a chute, and fill that coal bin with coal through the window put there just for that purpose. On the back wall, we stored split wood for the fireplace and water heating stove. In the open space were clothes lines where we dried our clothes in the wintertime. I remember being sent down to get something for supper from the 'cold' room and running back up real fast as it was really dark and scarey at night.

Upstairs were three rooms and a large bathroom.

> *Tredway*: I always stayed in the room at the top of the stairs. The door is to the left, just as you reach the top of the stairs.

Oh the green room. That was my room. When you were in the service you had a small leather satchel that when filled was quite round. One time when you were staying there and I was still in the crib, I dreamt that bag was a bear and it was chasing me. It was a very bad dream and I woke up screaming from it!! Mother was taking a bath at the time and took me in with her. This woke me up and calmed me down.

The room at the back of the hall was the yellow room. That was Mother and Daddy's but at the time Alice came there it was Owen's and Emeline's room. It had a birdseye maple bedroom set. twin beds, a big chest of drawers amd a smaller dressing table.

The other bedroom was in early years the purple room but later became the orange room. That room I believe was used as the guest room. It had a big four-poster bed that had been built by Benjamin Stacey Tredway, Owen's father. That antique bed had rope woven as a foundation for the mattress. Later a flat spring was added. The bathroom was right across the hall from that room.. I'm not at all sure which room mother stayed in while she lived there but I would guess the green room.

Brynhild Oas was Alice's longtime friend. Born in 1903, she was 96 when I interviewed her. They met when Alice was in high school and Byrnhilde was the librarian, about 1924 or so.

> *Brynhild*: The first I knew of your mother was when she was in high school. They had an art exhibit and they picked different kids to take part. How they did this art exhibit was by

"staging" the work of art. So mother was the girl in the staging of the "Song of the Lark". She was chosen to reinact, on stage, with special lighting, this painting. First someone would tell about the picture and artist. Then the curtain would open and there stood Alice pointing at the lark in the tree, like the original painting. It was very accurate only, of course, much larger than the painting. I was really impressed with how well she "acted" the picture.

This is about all I know about Mother during her high school years, 1923 to 1927, when she graduated from high school. But, the story picks up from here with the letters she saved from her years away at college and teaching from 1927 to 1932 when she married Daddy.

As a piano tuner for 30 odd years, I've talked to many people. Sometimes when describing something in my life I would refer to the fact that my father was 44 years older than my mother. Several of these people said, "How romantic, a May-September marriage. You should write a book about that, it's really interesting." So, that was what first put the idea in my head for writing this story. My mother always talked about how she put herself through school so the references to money that Owen gave her, I assume was just extra spending money.

All that I know about the romance is from the following letters. I've edited these to simplify the story. Even though Daddy resists Mother's suggestion for marriage, because of his age, I believe they had fallen in love.

These letters are signed "Daddy T, ORT, Daddy, T," etc. and they are all Owen R. Tredway, my father.

College Years

O. R. Tredway | Estb'd 1896 | Oscar E. Ole

TREDWAY'S PHARMACY
Munising, Michigan

October 20, 1927

Dear Alice

Your three letters have been duly received, and we are more than pleased to hear that you are so happy and getting along so well in your work.

I have just returned to the store from church, and will be here till dinner time as usual.

Mrs. McFayden is taking care of us in good shape, altho we miss you in a great many ways.

Mrs. Tredway has failed since you saw her. She can't walk alone, and it is hard for her to get up and down stairs. When we do get her down in morning she stays till bedtime.

I take her out every day for a ride but the snow will soon come and then we can't go anymore. We miss you on our rides—you saw everything as we passed along. The trees were beautiful this fall. I haven't brought home any trees yet, and don't think I will till spring. It doesn't seem the right time now, and they would soon be covered with snow and we couldn't see them 'till spring anyhow.

Marie's [Owen's niece] little girl Barbara Jean came Oct. 13th and they are doing fine. You haven't said anything about your eyes, they surely must be O.K. or you couldn't get up so early and study so long. We would be awfully glad to have you some week-end. I will speak to Mrs. Vendein amd see if some of them can't bring you. I see the girls are here every week.

I can imagine your talk on Munising, and am sure you would picture it in an interesting way. We enjoy your letters and would be glad to hear from you often. It is now one o'clock and I must go home. Hope the radio will come good this P.M. the evenings are so long now that it helps out.

Yours,
The Tredways

Nov. 9, 1927

Dear Alice,

I received your lovely letter, and was in hope you could come down last weekend. Since you didn't, I think you better come this weekend if you can.

Aunt Emeline has failed a lot this past week. She is in bed all the time now, and we have to feed her with a spoon as she can take only liquids. She just lays in sort of a stupor and does not move for hours. We had Dr. yesterday and he says she can't last long—There is a bus line between Marquette and Munising now or you could come on the train. Am enclosing check to pay your fare.

Sincerely,

O.R.T.

Janis: Emeline asked for Mother on her deathbed. I got the impression [from Mother] that she wanted Mother to take care of Daddy. When Emeline called for Mother, she was in school in Marquette and it took a while for her to get there. So when Mother finally got there, Emeline was already comatose and Mother never did find out what she wanted to say to her.

January 15, 1928

Dear Alice,

Mrs. Mac just phoned me (11:45 AM) and wanted to know if I would go to the hotel for my dinner. She is not feeling very well…

Received your last two very interesting letters, which I am trying to answer.

I wonder what Mrs. Younquist wants to see me about. If I should go up this week, will call you up.

Hope Myrtle is over the operation and doing well. Am enclosing a check for $10.00 so you will have enough to get some shoes.

Yours Sincerely,

O R T

I've included this letter from Clara as it is chronologically accurate and brings Clara [fourteen years old] into Alice's life story. Clara was an important part of Mother's life.

February 12, 1928
(Written from 384 Lincoln, Oklahoma City, Okla.)

Alice (*l*) and Clara (*r*)

Dear Sister Alice,

Well I got a letter from you at last. My first one since I left Michigan.

We never knew Myrtle's children were sick. Say, thats hard. First Myrtle with appendicitis then Vivian, then Dorothy with the measles. What was the matter with Vivian? Did she have measles too ...?

So Mr. O.R. Tredway went to Florida after all. I suppose he'll be back after winter is over or will he?

You asked me what time we go to bed. Well we go to bed about somewhere between 8 and 10. We get up somewhere between 6 and 7. We have lots of sleep, but it's hard to sleep in the front seat of the "old Chev." George has slept in the back seat since we came to O.K. [Oklahoma?] City, come to think of it, the last time I've slept in a bed or where I could stretch out, was the second of November, four months ago.!!!

James is working for the fellow that owns these camps, R.H. George. Our George and Dad are putting in the basement in a root house or cyclone cellar. Mother is cleaning cabins so they're all busy 'cept me. That leaves me housekeeper and chief cook and bottle washer. Ha Ha. Of course they all work except me. I just lay around the house. You know , You know. I wish this old cafe here would open, then I could get a job too....

Well how are you getting along in Normal? I hope you are getting along fine. Hoping you and Myrtle are feeling fine and dandy. I am your loving sis, Clara.

Don't be so long about writing this time. "Adios"

Feb, 13, 1928

Dear Alice,

Received your letter this morning and was sure glad to get it. … In fact am always glad to get your letters, altho you have so little time. I know you just have to steal it when you write me.

Well, I have had a nice trip and time since leaving Munising. I stayed all nite at Mackinaw City and arrived in G. R. [Grand Rapids] the next day at 4:45 P M and John [Haglund, Marie's husband] met me in the station. I had a short visit with him and then took the bus for Casnovia, [the small community where Owen grew up and where his mother still lived in their home.] which arrived in about an hour. Tredway and Ann were right there at the bus waiting. Barbara is the sweetest baby ever and prettier than any of the others. I stayed there Friday night, Saturday and Sat. nite, leaving Sunday P M at 4:30 on the bus for G. R. All I could get on the Pullman was an upper, which I didn't want but as I was anxious to be on the way, I took it, thinking perhaps I could get a lower at Detroit. After I got on the train a woman came in and was looking for #9 lower. Well I had #9 upper so she sat down and we began to talk. I introduced myself to her by giving her my card and she then gave me hers and said that she was from Muskegon and worked in a Dept. Store as floorwalker and educational instructor. As we became more acquainted I found her to be very interesting ... said she was all excited over the trip, (she was going to Miami.) Well, we had a very pleasant time to Jacksonville where we had to part. Arrived here Tuesday P M. Mr . Wade met me, so I was soon at my destination. Am staying here with the Wades. … We went for a drive yesterday out along the Hillsboro river. I thought of you and wished you could of been along, it was such a beautiful scene, the Sycamore trees along the river covered with spanish moss hanging down over the water. It is so different from the scenes up there.

Last Thursday I went to the Fair, which is a big thing here. It was on for eleven days. I wish you could have seen the fruit and vegetables. The displays were wonderful. There was so much to see that I can't begin to tell you all. A polo game was going on in front of the grand stand between two teams called Michigan and New Jersey and Michigan won. You may know that pleased me. As this was Shrine day the Shriners were there enmasse with their fezzes on. I went to the ceremonial in the evening and saw the novices initiated. After that we went to the ball and looked on. It was 1 o'clock when we got home.

I don't know what to say about your keeping on at school. I guess you will have to decide that, or at any rate it is quite aways ahead and we can talk it out when I return.

The weather is fine, am in my shirt sleeves and the door is open.

We were looking for Lindy [Charles Lindbergh] this morning, he was supposed to fly over here on his way to St. Louis from Havana, but we didn't see him. On the 22nd they are going to dedicate an airport here and expect to have 90 planes from all parts of the country, so I expect to see a lot of air stunts that day.

Well Alice I guess you will be tired of all this, so will quit.

With love, O R T

Am enclosing some clippings which I think are good.

A. M. WADE
MEMBER
TAMPA REAL ESTATE BOARD
TAMPA BOARD OF TRADE

PHONE 84-527

WADE'S REAL ESTATE OFFICE
CORNER BAYSHORE AND INTERBAY BOULEVARDS
BALLAST POINT

TAMPA, FLORIDA

Feb. 23rd, 11:00 am

Dear Alice,

You are probably wondering where the check is. Well I forgot to put it in, so you will get a letter sooner than you would otherwise.

Yesterday we were out at the airport and saw 40 planes in action, which was real interesting.

Am going to a bridge party tonight. …

Hope you are enjoying your new home. I have a nice room facing the south and can lie in bed and see the sun rise and listen to the mockingbirds sing each morning. Also have light at the head of my bed on a small stand like the one I have home between the beds so you can think of me each night lying in bed reading.

Am enclosing a leaf or two from a camphor tree, (crush them and you will smell camphor) which I took from a tree in our yard, also a Japanese Hibiscus. I made a list of the trees and plants in our yard and found there was over 50. Will show it to you when I get home.

The mail just came and your lovely letter was among it. Am so sorry that I forgot the check, for three cents won't go far and you will be more lonesome and homesick with out money. But you are resourceful and will make out some how that I won't worry.

Well, my dear, can't think of any more to write so bye, bye.

With love, Daddy T

Tampa March 5, 1928

My Dear Alice,

Have received two letters since writing you, and want to say was more than pleased to know of your perfect exam in Physiology and Hygiene. Will enclose the note because you value it so highly that you will want to keep it.

I have been running around quite a lot. We made one trip to Lake Wales (75 miles one way). There were about one hundred in the motorcade, mostly women. We saw I think, the most beautiful spot in Florida. It was the Bok Bird Sanctuary endowed by Ed Bok, editor of the Ladies Home Journal.

It consists of forty acres and is covered with all kinds of trees and shrubbery which was brought from different parts of the country. Also artificial lakes and everything interesting to lovers of nature. I know you would of been all excited over it.

We had our dinner in a rustic restaurant made of logs and called The Hitching Post. I took a picture of it. I also made a picture of some Flamingo, you can see these, when I came home.

A week ago yesterday, we (I mean the Wades) went to Sarasota, sixty miles away, and visited the winter quarters of the Ringling Circus. There were thirty eight elephants, twenty camels, twenty five zebras, three giraffe, lions tigers and every kind of animal you ever heard of. We spent two hours there, and then went over to the beach on the Gulf, and watched the bathers.

On the way down, we stopped at Bradenton and I called on Marguarite Leiphardt Hill, whom I have known since she was a little girl.

Yesterday, Mr. Wade and I went to church. It was a little Baptist Church, but it was full, and everyone seemed to be having a good time; we did.

Oh! yes. Mrs. McFayden's daughter and husband called to see me Saturday and asked me over to St. Petersburg for the next week-end, so I am expecting to go.

It isn't dark down here until 7 o'clock so you see we have more daylight here, being nearer the equator.

I didn't taste the candy, so can't tell how good it was, but if you could of seen the booth at the Fair where it was sold, I thought it was a meat market!!

I have been here four weeks and it doesn't seem half that long. Mrs. Wade is a fine cook and we have good eats, in fact, too much some of the time. She is taking a course two nights a week for eight weeks in Home Economics.

Was out this morning and played a round of golf, all alone. Have been out four or five times, but my back gives out. Hope it will get better for I do like to play golf.

Love, O.R.T.

Munising , Mich. 4/19/28

My dear Alice,

I think you had better wait a week before you come. We hope the weather and roads will be better by that time. Everyone says, "you had better of stayed in Florida a while longer." I guess so too. There was a foot of snow to wade thru this morning but I don't think I mind it so much as do the folks who have had to be in it all winter.

Haven't had the car pumped up and greased yet. If you come next week I will try and drive you back.

Love,
O.R.T.

Sometime in the early 1900's, Chan Brown homesteaded a parcel of land, one mile square, on Lake Superior, seventeen miles west of Munising. I'm not sure how Owen knew him, but the property centered on the rocky river mouth of the Rock River, a small river winding along the road from Chatham. There was another couple, the Henry Freemans, who also were friends. Daddy and Henry Freeman built a cabin, right on the beach by Lake Superior. After their cabin on the river burned in the 30's, the Browns and Braamses (Edna Braamse is Chan Brown's daughter,) added on to this beach cabin and also used it.

The Henowen cottage.

This cabin was called HenOwen after these two men. As children we spent much time there and were the same age as the Braamse children. In the 50's this cabin burned. I still spend time there in one of the many other cabins at this beach resort. and enjoy the Braamse family. Owen and Emeline spent time with Chan and his wife there. They called this place "Rock River."

Munising, May 20th, 1928

Dear Alice—

I have received and digested your last two letters and of course am sorry of your partial failure in teaching. I still think you will come out all right if your health and eyes hold out, for you are determined to make a success.

You may know that I have been busy this week, but we always have something to be thankful for. The fire might have been much worse. The insurance will cover part of the loss. The lower story was not burned so I plan to rebuild at once . C.B.[Chas. Brandt?] and A & P want to come back to the old location. They think it the best in town. [Daddy must have owned this building at that time. It held two stores, Brandt's Appliance and A & P Grocery.]

Guess I will drive up to Rock River this PM and stay all night if it seems agreeable, after I get there.

Mrs. McFayden … asked me if I had made any plans. I told her you wanted to come, so she said, well, I will be over Monday and see you again ... I don't know what she has in view. You can depend on coming just as we have talked at any rate …

Monday-

Stayed all nite at Rock River. Drove back early this morning. The leaves are beginning to come out and things are looking so pretty and green....The Browns went to Gladstone to meet Edna.; They expected her on the 5am train this morning so I was alone this morning. …

Love, T

Mrs. McFayden is the housekeeper that helped out in the Tredway's household. I think Alice is concerned about the propriety of her staying in the house with Owen, with both of them being single, now that Emeline has passed on.

12:30 PM Fast time—Munising Mi. June 6, 1928

My Dear Alice-

Mrs. McFayden was just in to see me. She will be at the island 'til July 1st. Then she wants to have a room at my house and do some sewing. So you see it will be all right for you to come. I told her what you had said about coming, so she understands conditions. After you are here we can talk it all over and if you want to do something else you can.

After reading your nice long letter it changed things so. I have been waiting to know what to write you. After Mrs Mc talked with me I felt that I could write you at once and have you come when school is out.

Haven't time to write more as it is dinner time now. Let me know what day you will want to come—and it may be so I can go after you.

Love, T

Tuesday Nite 9:30 at store—after 6/6/28

Dear Alice,

If you hadn't been such a good girl to write often in the past, am afraid I would feel like scolding a bit. We looked for a letter every day after Tuesday, and it didn't come till Saturday.

You know we were anxious because everything was so different this time. Well it is alright now, and we hope to see you Saturday. Wish you could come Friday nite for you will have to leave again Sunday 1:30.

Hope everything is going fine with you. Molly [housekeeper?] has been having a cold and hasn't been out of the house for two days, and that is pretty hard for her. Well, will see you soon so will close and go home and play the radio.

love, T

When Mother went to school in Marquette, she "lived in" with the Shriners and helped with their baby, Zoe, and with the housework, for her room and board. Evidently from this letter, the Shriners moved to Indiana after that first year at school.

1616 South Center Street
Terre Haute, Indiana

September 24, 1928

Dear Alice,

While Mrs. Shriner is rocking little Zoe to sleep, I'll endeavor to acquaint you with the events that have taken place since we left the "Great Northern Woods."

... Zoe seemed to enjoy riding all day in the Ford on our way down. We had the back seat and the space between the seats filled with 'stuff' almost to the roof of the car. ... She can walk now and says quite a few words ... When you have time to write, we should be delighted to know what program you have elected for the fall term and how you have enjoyed your summer vacation. We enjoyed our visit with you and Mr. Tredway very much. It would have been a shame not to have visited Munising and had a glimpse of Miner's Castle before we left the Upper Peninsula.

... Trusting that you will have a glorious year and that you will refrain from working all night on your lessons, I am

Most sincerely,

Walter Shriner

There is a big space of time here because Owen and Alice didn't write unless she was at school or Owen was in Florida.

Office of
GEO. C. HIGBEE
OFFICIAL COURT STENOGRAPHER
MARQUETTE, MICH.
Feb. 17, 1929

My dear Miss Halstead,

We are just home from a work a day trip of seven weeks, and so only today was I able to take care of my SS class. But, I did not see you there!!!

It is the greatest satisfaction to me to have you present in the class and may I confidently look for you next Sunday?

The Topic— "Christian Growth."

References John1/40-42 Matt16/15-18
Luke 2/40, 52 John21/15-19
Eph.4/11-16 Phil.1/6, 9-11
Col. 1/9-11 Heb 6/1-3
Golden Text—-2Peter 3/18

Sincerely yours,

Geo. C. Higbee

Feb. 27, 1929

Have been looking for a letter every day but won't wait any longer. Received you post card before leaving home. The scene did remind me of a spot I well remember, not far from Munising.

I left home Friday the 25th as planned, stayed the night at Mackinaw City arriving at Grand Rapids the next day. Stayed two nights at Maries. Took the Pullman Monday night at 6:35. Marie went to the station with me. Had a nice time there and the children were delighted to see me. From G. R. the trip was not so pleasant as last year as I didn't find anyone to visit with. There was a woman across the aisle from me and I tried to talk with her but she would just answer my questions and that was all, guess she was afraid of me.

Well I got here as per schedule and Mr. Wade met me at the station. Have been going somewhere every day, and haven't had time to get my Ford out. The big fair is over and have been to that twice. Played golf twice with Mr. Wade. We are going to St. Petersburg today. Might see Sam Mark over there. [Sam Mark & Sons was a dry goods store on the northwest corner of downtown Munising at that time.] The weather is fine, just like July in the U.P. We had a picnic dinner in the park Saturday and it reminded me of last summer when we had ours on the shores of old Lake Superior.

Hope everything is going well with you. Haven't got rid of my cold which came on when you were home. Marie said, "Must have gotten it from her." Well I said "I wasn't close enough to her to catch it, do you think I was close enough to Alice?" Well she said " I don't know but she might have been close enough to you."

love,
Daddy Tredway

5601 Bayshore Blvd
Tampa, Fla.

March 1, 1929

Dear Alice,

The first airplane carrying mail out ot Tampa will leave here at 1:30 today, and the Postmaster wants to have a record load for them, so they are appealing to everybody to write. So, I am going to add three to the number and you will be delighted to receive a letter by air, part of the way at least, for I suppose it will land at Detroit or Chicago.

Received your valentine with the dear verse—for which I thank you ... and I just received your last letter posted Feb. 25 which I have just finished reading, as I also got one from Oscar…you might know that I am quite happy, have been playing golf the last two P.M.'s and got up a good score of 40 on one round, pretty warm here now 84. Have been to two bridge parties and am invited to another Sat. nite. They have all been on Sat nite so you know what that means for my bath.

I have my sleeves rolled up and I am so warm that my arms stick to the desk while I am writing. Mrs. Wade has gone to a party and Mr. Wade is getting lunch for us. Warner, the boy will soon be home from school. Yesterday I was in an orange grove and saw and smelled the orange blossoms. Wish I could send you some of the fragrance. Last night we went to a neighbors to hear the big fight on the radio. Didn't think it was very exciting … Can't write more, haven't time,

Love, Daddy T

CELEBRATION TO START AIR MAIL TODAY

Tampa Letters To Go to New York in 18 Hours

Air mail service will be inaugurated here this afternoon at 1 o'clock at the airport where postal, aircraft and city officials, business and others will assemble to participate in the ceremonies celebrating the event.

The first plane will leave here promptly at 1:25 o'clock for Daytona Beach, where it will connect with the air mail route to New York and other points throughout the country. Inauguration of the service will give Tampa an 18-hour mail connection

Wednesday Mar. 13th, 1929 10:30A

Dear Alice,

My pen went bad, so had Oscar [the other pharmacist who was a partner at Tredway's Drug store and later bought my dad out.] send me another. Wade's had some signet green ink so I have changed my color. As our mail comes about this time every day, I may get a letter from you this morning. Had one from Oscar yesterday telling of the blizzard you had last week.

... This week Monday when I came home from playing golf about 6 PM, Mrs Wade says, "your girl was here to see you." Which one? I said, "Oh, Mrs. Mac". she said, "She was here about eight minutes ago." She left a card with her address, Mary MacFayden ...., so I don't know whether I will see them or not.

Am glad you don't feel the nervousness anymore when teaching. Was sure you would over come it. Am wondering what your surprise will be. Guess it will be a photo from what you say about recognizing it.

Hope you received the check OK. Sorry I addressed my letter wrong. Have had one letter from sister[Ella] and one from Marie. They are quite happy and are planning to get a new Ford in the spring. I hope they will, then they can get out and have a good time and go to Casnovia, week-ends ... Only two more weeks and then you will have to begin to plan for next term. You haven't said anything about it. Wonder what you will do vacation week? If I were home you would come to Munising I am sure.

The mail just came, but no letters so will look for one tomorrow. Yesterday I went to see a chicken ranch. Went around with the keeper to gather the eggs. He keeps a record of each hen and egg on a chart over the nest. They have 1200 hens and get 600 or more eggs each day. They are all white leghorns and did look pretty. You would of enjoyed it, I know. He showed a rooster he paid $75.00 for. These pure bred hens never want to set. Eggs are $.45/dozen now.

I found one of my houses in bad condition. [Owen had rentals in Florida.] The roof had leaked and the plaster dropped off the ceiling in spots so had to have it patched and then painted. You can imagine how it looked after the work was completed. Well—I went out and *bought a mop for $.50 and spent 3 hours mopping the floor and cleaning the woodwork. The work didn't hurt me any. Didn't need to play golf that day!!!*

Well my dear, guess there isn't any more to tell. Oh, yes. Yesterday we went down to the Shrine Temple and bought two Indian blankets, one for the Wades and one for me. The shrine put on the sale to raise some money. They have 4000 to sell. I think you will like it. It will be nice to have in the car next summer. bye, bye,

Love, Mr. Tredway

FRANK SULLIVAN, 1st V.P.
VIOLET WHITE SMITH, 2d V. P.

A. M. WADE, PRES.

J. J. HALL, SEC.
MRS. J. DE LA GRANA, TREAS.

The Florida Archaeological Society

TAMPA, FLORIDA

Friday, March 15, 1929

Dear Alice,

Your letter received yesterday. In order you may get the check for sure on the 20th, will send it today. Guess you don't want to take any chances of my forgetting again. Well, my dear girl, I don't blame you for it must be a queer sensation to have when you are away from home and have only three cents and hungry. When you go home I think you had better forget to take your check book along, or your Dad will expect you to give him some—

Last night we three men, Mr. Wade, Warner and I, went downtown to the talkies. I enjoyed one of them very much. It was an Alaskan play, and the outstanding feature was a German Police Dog!! He was so intelligent that he seemed almost human.

Yesterday PM Mr Wade went with me to play golf. It was good and warm too, 83 degrees. You may know that I sweat good and plenty.

Mrs. Wade has got the vacuum here in the office and is beginning to clean up so I will have to move. Well nothing has happened since my letter written two days ago, so good bye.

Love,
Daddy Tredway

April Fool's Day—9:00 AM—4/1/29

My Dear Girlie—

Monday morning right after breakfast I am writing this. By the time you get it you will have been in school a week on the new and last term after having spent a very happy week with your dear mother and the rest of the family. I hope the weather was good. The paper here showed the temperature mild, in Detroit.

You have been so happy, am sure you didn't miss a letter from me last week, and you will be so busy with your new work this week that you won't have time to think of it—

Received the very nice Easter card with the beautiful verse. You are always sure to have words that mean something—Yes, and the picture. It is fine of you. I would think anyone would give you a job on it. Am sure that I would!! I have it on my dresser where I can see it this very moment.

... Lonesome, you aren't the only one. When I saw your picture I just wanted to see you so bad—am beginning to think about going home, it is so warm here now that I long for a whiff of the old Superior breeze.

... Now I'm going to read your letter and see if there is any thing for me to answer—don't forget to send or rather tell me your marks in the next letter here. Won't be here only two more Sundays. I forgot to tell you, we all got up yesterday morning at 4:30 and went to the Sunrise Easter Service at the park out of doors. It was a musical service as you will see by the program I am enclosing.

Now I will read the morning paper, wash my hair, then go and play a round of golf before it gets too hot.

bye bye,
With love, Daddy T.

Indian Rocks Beach
—On the Gulf—
30 miles from Tampa,
near Clearwater

Tuesday AM—April 9, 1929

My Dear Alice,

We rented this furnished cottage for a week and came out last Friday PM. Saturday, Mr. Wade and I went to Clearwater and played 18 holes of golf. We go in before breakfast every day and then again sometime in PM. [Swimming, I assume].

It is wonderful here. I am writing this out on the screened porch overlooking the gulf—The cottage is about the same distance from the water as our cottage at Rock River. The nearest cottage is a block away. Am in my knickers without shoes or sox. Temperature is 85 degrees with a nice cool breeze all the time and you need a blanket at night.

... I have often wanted to spend some time on the gulf and you bet I'm enjoying it. Wish you were here to share it. Don't think the old bathing suit will be much good when the week is up.

A week ago today I drove to Manatee and spent the night at Margarites. The baby was just 2 months old and as you know, about all the talk was baby. Well, I had a good time anyhow. She went out in the chicken coop and caught a nice pullet and we had fried chicken for dinner.

Daddy in Florida.

I am reading Pilgrims Progress out here ... presuming you have read it long ago.

I expect to start home next week . Probably about the 17th. Have been getting your letters on Thursday each week so don't send any more here unless they reach here by that time. Am going to Detroit first and stay over Sunday with Mae and Jo. Then to Grand Rapids for a day or so and if my sister is at Casnovia, will go up there for a day or two. So you see, that will bring me home the last of April or 1st of May—

Will send you a check sometime before May 1st. ... Will let you know later how fast I am going. ... Hope to see you pretty soon after I get home, and it will be a grand and glorious reunion!!!!!

Love Daddy T.

The only negative thing mother ever said about Daddy, was that he was tight-fisted with his money. I think maybe he questioned her spending habits and she sent back his check that he refers to in the next letter.

1:30 at Home, May 1st, 1929

My dear Alice,

I am simply dumfounded after receiving your check Monday morning. I couldn't imagine why you had sent it so soon. Then your letter this morning. As this is the 1st of May, I had to make out bills and I just couldn't think of anything, only you, and wondered what I did so awful. Guess I made a mess of everything.

I think you are even with me now, for I have been very unhappy ever since your letter came, and I just couldn't go back to the store till I wrote you. Now, My Dear, I didn't intend to say anything that could be interpreted as you have taken it, and I am extremely sorry that you have been unhappy on account of something I said. You know, I haven't asked you to make any statement and have only asked you about some things which I thought would be in a fatherly way. And now you say you won't come home "till I come after you-".

I don't think you know how that sounds to me. You ought to know me better Alice than to allow yourself to get so worked up over it. I have always given you money when you needed it and will continue, too.

Haven't time to write more now. Eva [his hired salesgirl?] is taking her vacation so I will be busy.

Love, Daddy T.

Munising, Mich. June 2, 1929
10:30 AM At the store

Dear Al—

Have just finished posting my books and haven't anything to do till dinner time, only wait for customers, and they are very scarce.

Received your letter yesterday morning at the store. While I went to Rock River Friday PM, I don't think you saw me for I left here right after dinner and went via Forest Lake. Guess you had a vision. Mr. Drury invited me to stay and have tea, so we had a nice visit over the tea and I was home by 9 o'clock.

It was so cold last nite that I couldn't take my bath. But I'll fire up today and make some hot water. [The hot water tank was part of the heating system so if the furnace didn't run, the house had no hot water.]

Daddy

[All the time we grew up, he was "Daddy", as Mother called him that, and so did we.]

Thursday AM 9:45

Dear Alice—

Your letter was waiting for me again this morning. I did answer your other letter Sunday, but haven't sent it . Will enclose it with this.

... If you want to go to Ishpeming [where sister Myrtle lived] before coming home, I think your plan is best, for me to go after you Sunday. Could leave here at eleven our time and that would get me there by twelve your time. Am sorry you have been feeling ill, but

you are better now. Am in such a hurry that you won't be able to read this I guess. The car is out in front waiting for me, and wants to go. You can write again so I will know definitely what to do.

Love, Daddy

Munising, June 12, 1929
9:30 Potato Time [Must be a private joke]

Dear Alice,

Just came home and will spend the rest of the evening with you. It was so cold in the house that I built a fire in the furnace today noon after I had my dinner, and it is nice and warm now. The radio is playing on WLW and I am in a good mood, happy to know that it won't be long till my little girl will be here for company.

Your letter was at the store at nine o'clock. I then had to wash the car, and you know it was muddy.

The painters began work Monday but haven't showed up today. All they have done is to prepare the walls. Hope they will come tomorrow ... You will find a pretty dirty house to come home to, but after things are cleaned up it will be lots nicer. I mowed the grass today on your back yard ... 'member you said you would do it. Can't think of any more news so guess will have to quit.

Love, Daddy

Now it is summer and Alice is in Munising, and we will not hear more until Owen leaves for Florida the next winter, except for the following letter from Shriners, the first family she stayed with in Marquette.

Sunday Evening
June 15, [1929?]

Dear Alice,

'Tis disgusting the way I have procrastinated writing my thanks to you for the fragrance of cedar sent from the north woods. 'Twas dear of you to think of us and want to add to our holiday cheer.

And now you write to us and invite us to visit you. Thank you so much. We shall be delighted to stop for a few hours or over night if possible ....

Our baby girls are mighty sweet and well. Zoe Marjorie does not wish to be called baby . She says,"Me no baby, me a big girl," and she is though sister is only eight pounds smaller!!

We are glad to hear you have a position for next year. When you return for your last years work at school you will get a great deal out of the studies though you may feel less a part of class and school.

... It may be a week or more before we reach Marquette for we are visiting friends and relatives on the way.

Until then, Lovingly, Virginia Shriner

The following letter shows of Alice's search for spirituality even as a young girl of 20.

TRINITY METHODIST EPISCOPAL CHURCH
LAKE DRIVE AND CALKINS AVENUE
GRAND RAPIDS, MICHIGAN

MINISTER
JOHN S. TREDENNICK

MINISTER OF FINANCE
JOHN R. GREGORY

Jan. 16-30

Dear Miss Halstead,

I am much interested in your letter and plans. There are all too few who are really seeking to know and do The Master's will.

From what you tell me, I gather you are not sure of His will. Then I should go on with the work you have thus far prepared yourself for— Teaching—. Pay your obligation and wait for the Lord to open the doors along the way as he surely will.

Rarely do we discern God's will apart from the doing day by day that which He leads— Therefore, 1930 may be a year rich in blessing to you, both in your work and life.

Your Brother in Christ, John S. Tredennick

6204 Bayshore Blvd.
Tampa, Fla.

Jan.22, 1930

Dear Alice

The sun is shining and it is just as nice and warm as one could wish. I can't imagine there is two feet of snow anywhere. It wouldn't last long here.

I stayed at Marie's one night and arrived here yesterday.

Have a nice place to stay but miss the Wades. This house is next door to the Davis house where we stayed three winters, but is much better in every way. Will take a picture of it to show you when I return. Am going to see about my Ford today, then I can get around and do something.

Hope you are getting along fine at school and not worrying anymore. I sent my golf clubs by mail and they haven't come yet. Hope they come tomorrow as I am getting anxious to play. My cold is better and will be alright in a few days, I think. You can write me at above address for a while.

Love, Daddy

Sunday afternoon-2:00PM, on the beach.
Feb. 1930?

My dear girl,

Your last letter written in bed at 12 o'clock last Sunday night was a hard letter for you to write because you didn't say some things that you were thinking. Well you are a good sport anyway.

Went to church this morning, then to my room and read the paper, and now I am sitting in my old Ford on the beach not more than 50 feet from the water's edge. A very strong nor'wester is blowing and the waves are rolling the highest I have seen here, although they are no larger than I have seen on Old Superior. The sun is shining bright but the wind is so strong that it makes the old car rock.

Last Monday nite, when I came home from the show-9:30- the living room (I have to go through it) was full of people playing bridge (at tables). Mrs. Davis approached me and said one of her guest didn't come and would I fill in. I reluctantly consented-Well anyhow I got in on the eats, orange juice, strawberries and cream on angelfood cake and coffee. Not so bad.

Had a letter from Marie and she said "John had a characteristic letter from Alice and that settled things in her favor!"

Sitting here looking over the water reminds me of our picnic grounds, minus the beautiful rocky shore, picnic dinner, and good company. I have the "American" which I am going to read later, but you won't be able to hear me.

I'll bet you are having some winter weather up there now, or we wouldn't be having this wind. Yesterday it rained all day. Hope I can go out tomorrow and golf. Have met three men who I played with last year on this course and so we have a foursome when we are all there at the same time.

... Not many out here today, only those who want to see a rough sea. Parked ahead of me are four women who have just gotten in their car, coats all up around their necks just like they would be in Michigan today.

Wish I had a glass of that good buttermilk right now, the kind you churn. I buy it often here but I'll bet yours is better. I use the shower bath here. It is so nice to wash my hair. Guess you will be glad for a regular bath by spring.

Love, Daddy

This may be Owen's response to Alice requesting they be married.

Tuesday 3PM 3/11/30

My Dear Alice,

I intended to go to a ball game at this time, Detroit vs. Brooklyn, but it has been cloudy all day and began to rain a few minutes ago so I have to stay in, and will pass the time with you.

Yesterday I played golf. When I returned home your letter and the

Munising News was waiting for me, so that was enough for the rest of the evening.

I am indeed glad you did so well before your class and didn't get nervous. I am sure you will be all right when you get out teaching. You say I am so calm and gentle. The reason is, I don't want to hurt you, but I think it will be best if I do say something. I can't go on like this. Was in hopes you wouldn't say any more about it. Unless you promise not to tease me any more I think I shall stay here, for it worries me and makes me unhappy. I have made up my mind and you know how stubborn I am. You know my reason so please don't.

Clara seems to be out of luck. Well, am glad she has found a place What was the matter at Dobbs?

You have been home [to the farm] and had a good time over the week-end. Hope you are happy, and had a good visit with George .... What are you going to do during your vacation? ... I thought you would of waited and gone home then.

We have our dinner at 6 PM and am so full all the evening that I don't want even an orange.. So you have been eating apples all alone each night, but I have grapefruit every morning and they are delicious. We pick them off the Fishers own trees. Mrs. Fisher washes my silk underwear and golf socks. She won't send them in the wash.

love, Daddy

Sunday, March 30, 1930

Alice Dear,

Went to M.E. Church this morning. Came home read the Sunday paper till dinner was ready, [at]2 o'clock. And what do you think we had? My favorite meat, you know what that is, and it was sure good. After dinner went for a ride, with Todd (the Fischer boy) over to the beach and around town. The evening was spent sitting around visiting, of course my reading is done in bed, after which I think of you and go to sleep.

I commenced [to read?] les Miserables when I first came here, and read a little each night when it isn't too cold. You will laugh when

I tell you that I had to have a hot water bottle to my feet about six nights. Didn't need one at home did I?

Will finish the book in another week or so. Jean Valjean is right now in the sewer. I think it a wonderful book. Marius & Cosette are real lovers.

Monday, March 31st

This my regular golf day. I go right after lunch, drive 12 miles and play 18 holes. Had a partner today, and after we finished went into the clubhouse for a drink of Coca-Cola and came out and started home. After I had gotten halfway home, I noticed that my clubs were missing. Had left them on the porch of the clubhouse. Well, I just turned round and went back and they were right where I left them. Well, that made me late for dinner, as it was 7 o'clock when I got back, and Mrs. Fischer, like all women, was worrying for fear some accident had happened—That finished another day.

Bye-

Tuesday, April 1st

As you are having such a nice time this week at Limestone with your kin, am going to tell you every day what I am doing. This PM, went to St. Pete and called on my friends the Messengers. Was there 3 hours. She served lemonade with 3 strawberries in it and a piece of delicious cake she had just made. After starting home I stopped at the depot to see Ted, (Mrs. Davis' son) and while there his wife drove up. You saw her last summer at Rock River, so we had a few minutes to visit before I had to leave for home.

It was 6 o'clock then, so when I came in the house, I saw a letter on my plate; Mrs Fisher said, "there is a nice fat letter for you". As dinner was ready, I put the letter in my pocket. After we finished, I went to my room where I could be alone and opened your letter. Do you know there was one whole sheet of paper that didn't have a scratch on it? So I guess that was April Fool for me!! It was a good letter never the less. You certainly had a strenuous week with your exams and all and Mrs. Zerbel [where Alice is living in Marquette now] was indeed good to you. Hope you will get a good mark....

Your wardrobe must be pretty well depleted. Well, my dear, whatever you really need, I want you to get. You are using so much for transportation that I am afraid you haven't much else left.

bye

Wednesday, April 2nd

This is my regular golf day. Went earlier than usual today as I wanted to go in to Tarpon Springs to make arrangements for a trip up the river I'm going to take tomorrow, which I will tell you about in tomorrow's chronicles. Played alone today. Had a fairly good game, made 58 and 56 and had a few good drives of 200 yds. Have lost all of those balls I brought. Bought one at the clubhouse for 15 cents and lost that, so I saw two boys fishing balls out of a water hazard and I bought 15 for $1.25. So, I think that ought to be enough to last while I am here. Was home at 5:30 today, and stayed in all evening.

Haven't been to a show since last Friday. I think your writing is all right and I wouldn't take it again.

bye

Thursday, Apr. 3rd

Mrs. Fischer and I left the house today at 12 o'clock right after lunch, in my Ford for Tarpon Springs, where we took a launch ride, starting at 1 o'clock up the Anclote river, 15 miles into the jungle. It reminded me of our trip down the Taquamenon and was just as crooked, but the scenery was real tropical. Where we landed they had a dead alligator in the edge of the water with a rope around him so he wouldn't float away, for the tourists to see. I thought it a good joke as I have seen three at different times on the golf course alive!!! Well, it was a beautiful trip anyway the day was perfect. Sun shining and just enough breeze to be comfortable, with my head hatless, and sleeves rolled up and linen knickers. On our return after landing we had a bottle of pop, then went to the Church of the Good Shepherd to see the Inness paintings, and listen to a woman lecture on them which was very interesting. I know, from the way she looked and the motions she made, and everybody seemed to be so interested....I didn't hear a word of it—Am enclosing a card about it. [My father was very hard of hearing by this time in his life. He had a hearing aid which helped.] We arrived home at 5:30 and am writing all this on my knee.

bye

Friday Apr. 4th

Got up an hour earlier than usual this morning to go deep sea fishing, way out in the gulf, for kingfish. It had been raining during the night and was cloudy and didn't look —good—

Mrs. Fisher had breakfast ready and a lunch for me to take along. The boat was to leave at 8:30 AM. I was at the dock, 15 minutes ahead of time, but the captain said 'it didn't look good to him, so he wouldn't go.' So I loafed around till lunch time, then went out to the golf course and played a round of golf with a man from Kentucky. Went to a show in the evening with Mr. Fisher and Todd—Read a few chapters and went to sleep.

bye

Saturday Apr. 5th

We intended to go to Tampa today and come back tomorrow, but it rained hard all day. So we had to stay around the house and read. The only thing of interest was your letter which came at 2 o'clock. I wasn't looking for it, as I supposed you were out home, but instead you were a very unhappy girl because your stingy old daddy didn't send enough money.

Well, I'm sorry Alice, but I feel sure that you went home anyway, for you know that I would want you to. Am glad you want to belong to the Tau Pau Nu, because I think it would help you in many ways. You haven't said what it costs but am going to send you, in this letter, a check, and I want you to join, and also get some clothes,

bye

Sunday Apr. 6th- 9:30 PM

Went to church. After dinner went for ride to New Port Richey—20 miles—Then we went to the beach and had lunch, ham (fried) sandwich, and coffee. Just got home and am writing this in bed. Will read a while and call it a day.

Nightie—

Monday morning
Last edition.

I think this is the longest letter I have ever written to you, and I guess the poorist written—

Right now (10:00 AM) you are at college registering. Now I will mail this epistle—

love from your old stingy Daddy

Clearwater-April 21- 1930

My Dear Alice-

By the time you receive this letter I will be on my way home. Expect to leave here Thurs. the 24th-will stop over Sunday with Marie and family, and arrive home sometime next week.

I want to see Dr. Hornberger soon as I can. Am not hearing so well as I did, so will be going to Marquette, perhaps on Friday and you can come home with me. Will write you definitely after I get home.

My tablet is all gone so am using this sheet of yours. I haven't much to tell you in this letter. I played golf 3 days last week and went to the beach two afternoons, bathing, all alone. Saturday I took the Ford over to Tampa and layed it up. Came back here yesterday, with the Fishers. I'm lonesome without the Ford, and will have to stick around the house or walk for the next three days. Am expecting a letter from you today at 2 o'clock, so won't finish this till later. Hope you won't disappoint me. I can feel it will be here.

2:30 PM

Well! Your letter didn't come but Clara's did. She seem to be up against a wall again. Hope she will find a place. She certainly seems to be out of luck. I just don't seem to be in a mood for writing, so will quit.

Love, Daddy

*Hello Daddy,**

I felt terribly restless tonight so I tho't it was because you were near. Lonesome Daddy. Seems impossible to wait until Friday. Are you really coming after me? When are you coming for me?

[Alice]

*[This letter was folded inside the next letter.]

April 30th

Dear Alice-

Arrived home yesterday and found everything OK. Am having the car serviced today and will plan on going to Marquette Friday afternoon. Will call at the house, and if you can come along will bring you back.

Didn't get any letter the last week before leaving, so don't know your plans for this week-end. Will be glad to see you anyway.

Love, Daddy

May 16,'30—12 o'clock

My Dear Alice,

Oscar just asked me when I was going to Marquette again. When I said Monday, "Well," he said, "I wanted to go up there to the Rotary meeting Monday and possibly Tuesday."

You may look for me Tuesday, same time and place. If I am not there Tuesday, will surely come Wednesday. My hearing is better and am glad of it. Stayed home last evening and would of been glad of your company.

Love, Daddy

May 22

Dear Alice,

Arrived home on schedule and picked up a nail somewhere so had a flat this morning. Am enclosing check for your coat, hat, and some extra. Hope you will continue to like the coat, and can find a hat that suits as well.

You had better look for me at the college Monday. Same place and time but don't wait after eleven.

Love, Daddy

Munising-May 24th

Dear Alice

Have just come from the Inn, wasn't hungry, so, didn't eat much of the chicken. We had quite a time getting home last Sunday. Bumped along till we got within a block of the Trenary road and the motor went dead. Discovered that the terminal wire running to the battery was broken owning to such rough road, so I decided to hail the first car and send to Trenary for help. I flagged the next car and when he got out of his car I found it was Oscar[his partner at the Drug Store], on his way home from Rapid River. Wasn't that luck?

So I got out my towline and he towed me to Trenary. Was there over an hour getting a new terminal. It was 9:30 when we left Trenary and 11:00 when I got home, so you see we didn't do much better than you did.

Mr Oliver from Rock River is in the Hospital. Was over to see him and while there called on Mr. Thornen, and Louis Peters, you remember he is keeper at Doe Lake. These men are all old men, around my age, only 3 years and I will be 70, and I can't expect to be here more than 8 years, 'cause at 75, I am an old man. To take a young wife your age who would be apt to bear me a child and me an old man who probably would never see the child only for a year or two. I don't see how it could be. I don't want one now, Alice, do you know that I am 44 years older than you, which is 40 years too much.

I would think of the difference in our ages every time we were in public, and to introduce you as my wife would be extremely embarrassing. We would be pointed out as that man who married that young girl (what an old fool) and your Father———You said once you would not want me while he was around. Oh! I have thought of everything and I would not be happy only the little time we could be alone. I will admit that we have been indiscreet but have committed no sin, that is what we haven't done, thank God. Whatever we did was because you wanted to make me happy. I have never given you any encouragement in fact have always tried to discourage you.

God will forgive us, I am sure. You needn't think I will ever love another woman, for I will promise not to ever marry.

I think it will be fine for you to go to Myrtles and have a good rest on the farm, and if you want a school in town somewhere, Mr. Lee will surely have some vacant places. And don't send me any money, it is yours. You will not suffer any more than I. Whatever we have done wrong, we will have to suffer for, and God will guide us in the future.

love, Daddy

Munising- 5:30 PM
Sunday, May 31,1930

Dear Alice,

You are probably out fishing again today. You had such wonderful luck last Sunday. Don't you see what a nice time you can have with a nice young man who can row you around—-

Yesterday I went to the cemetery and attended the Memorial services. The flowers on my lot looked nice, and the wild rose bush is coming along OK.

Yes, it was your birthday too....22—-3 times that is 66...and the more I think, the farther I am from doing the thing you want. There is no use for me to argue any more. You won't admit I am right. In the years to come you will see for yourself. I can't think of you other than my dear little girl—and I want to be just Daddy.

I won't be coming after you this time. I remember you saying the bus line went thru Rock. If so, you won't have any trouble getting there. Wish we had brought some of your things, those boxes for instance— or will Mac [Aunt Myrtles husband] come after you?

May God bless you, and I hope it won't be too long before I will see you.

love, Daddy

Munising, June 10th, 1930—9 PM

My dear hard-worked girl,

Have been to two stores looking for Crystal Wall Cleaner, and they both tried to sell me a substitute, so you had better get it there with enclosed dollar.

Oscar went away Sunday PM and you know what that means for me. Won't be back till next Monday or Tuesday. I ate dinner today at the hotel with Mr. G...who was on his way home from the Soo, where he was fined $3000 for selling liquor....

Sunday I took a little ride and went up to the cemetery. The plants are doing fine....Went to baccalaureate Sunday nite...enjoyed the band playing more than anything else.

Haven't had a customer since I started to write this and it is now 9:20, my regular time to close up, so will say bye bye,

Daddy

Teaching at Stambaugh

AFTER GRADUATING FROM Northern Michigan Normal College, Alice took a teaching job in Stambaugh, Michigan, which is near Iron River. She lived with a family named Christensen and after two more letters from Owen, I didn't find anymore. I think during this time Owen was encouraging Alice to find a young man her own age. I have quite a few letters from beaus during this time so will print some letters from one of them, to give you an idea of what she was experiencing.

Munising, Mich. Sept. 14 '30
10:30 AM Store

My dear Alice,

I mailed and registered your certificate to C. I. Clark Supt.—- Stambough Mich. yesterday. He ought to get it tomorrow. I would get it from him soon as you can so that it won't get lost. Friday PM. I went to the fair. Mr. Roberts, Oscar, and Sadie rode out with me. We went in the Grandstand and watched the races and enjoyed them. Two of the horses were owned in Crystal Falls. Yes, I thought of the times we had been at the fair together, and you ask if I am lonesome for you. Why do you ask me that when you are reading my thoughts every day, and how could I help being lonesome after having such a cheerful and loving body with me for two months. I just couldn't feel like getting the meal you outlined. I don't seem to want to cook anything In fact am not hungry for supper after having a good dinner.

Your ankle needs a good lot of massaging, would be glad to give you a rub. I wouldn't take out any insurance this year Alice.

Yes, I think your banking system is all right, especially for you so far out, altho you do get a kick out of making a deposit....

This is another of those perfect days, wish I could decide on something to do this PM. Maybe something will turn up after dinner. Yesterday was out and played a round of golf....

9:30 PM at home—

Well, the only thing I could think of to do was to go out to our old picnic grounds, it was so nice and warm. Was gone 3 1/2 hours, had a book along "The Wolf of Wall Street" and read for two hours, while listening to the lapping of the water. After returning home while sitting on the porch, I heard the phone ring (for a wonder) and Mr. McDonald asked me up to his house. to see some moving pictures of the gold mine in California in which I have invested. Guess I told you about it. The man I bought from was showing them....It was very interesting, and did intend to go to church, but didn't want to miss the pictures.

I'll bet you were out swimming today. Hope you had a good time at something anyway. I can't think of anymore to say. Hope you have a good week in school and like it better every week. Don't think I can get up there to see you this fall—

8:40 Sunday morning after breakfast—

Alice, I can't find the cover for the silver sugar bowl, do you know anything about it? I like to use that because I can't break it. Mr. Roberts goes to conference tomorrow, so I will have to hustle today for the money, we were short over a hundred dollars Saturday. You can buy a nice lamb wool fur coat for $50.00. Cowells and Oscar have them.

Bye, D.

Oct. 12, 1930

Dear Alice—

I could answer the most of your letter in two words, "No, Alice"________I enjoyed the day in your school very much and liked the way you work. Am convinced now that you will make a first class teacher.

I think the letter from Leslie sort of got you upset.

I wonder what you are doing this beautiful day. After dinner I think the best thing to do is to be out in the sunshine or woods.

This will be a pretty uninteresting letter. I can't put the words together or think of the things to say that will not make you lonesome and still sound well. Did you get your pen and corks? I have a General Electric radio, on trial, and can get things morning, noon, and nite. My sister will enjoy it. The old one is all right for you, since you don't care for one so much.

9:30

Am just home from church, Oscar and Sadie came in to try the radio and they like it real well, so I think will close the deal tomorrow.

Went for a ride around the loop, saw the car at Zerbels, as no one was in sight didn't stop.

Haven't been feeling very good lately, my old trouble bothers, and my ankle isn't well.

Sorry your dress is too long. I'd send it back for them to fix.

good nite Alice, love, Daddy

The letters from Owen to Alice end here. I'm assuming that she did not keep them. I know he also was really encouraging her to see young men and perhaps pursue a relationship with one of the young men she had in her life . The above letter talks about Leslie whose letters she saved. I remember while growing up, hearing about Leslie, whom she complained that he seemed overly interested in the physical side of relationship as you can see from the following letter.

Spring, 1928

Dear Alice ,

After knowing you for about eight months to speak to and for about one month as a friend may be altogether too short a period to try to understand a girl. In fact, some people say that to tell a girl you understand her is an insult to the girl. But then, if that has any truth, I must be a great admirer of you. I can't quite figure you out even superficially.

I have been trying real hard to do that very thing too, ever since you called me up that night and said you were lonesome. I was very happy to be invited and indeed always enjoy your company. I was sort of checked on, what I then considered a symbolizing of a friendship when you said, "I don't want you to, Leslie. Let's just be friends."

That night, as I wandered home, this sentence sort of haunted me. I wondered if I had or was a degenerate to the extent of no longer knowing how to act. I finally decided that the trouble was caused by me—my standard of the measuring of the symbol was different from yours. I sort of intended to apologize, but decided that it would be just as well if I accepted your standard and said nothing.

A couple of nights later, I received a sharp refusal to attend an evening event—and this sort of reinforced my belief in my first analysis. The next was the trip to Sugar Loaf. That day I had a glorious time trying my best all the time to show you that I liked you in a way you would like. It is one of those few days in a lifetime I won't soon forget. I too was Sitting on Top of the World that Sunday. Then came the party Friday night. I had a lovely time at the party. Then the note. (I will always save it.) How proud I was to think I had filled a place in your mind as a friend. No compliment could have been greater as I know your ideals of a friend are high ....

But later down by the lake I again was more than human not to say I was not myself but another. [He must have tried to kiss her.] That set me to thinking again. How peculiar after my mind was all settled just a short time before. I wondered if it was just spontaneous or if you had taken my standard of friendship or if you were trying to show me that I could be more than a friend. I was happy but so wrapped up in my own thoughts that the walk home must have been very uninteresting.

Then again today, I am at sea. I couldn't in any way show that I cared for you in a way you would know. I did decide in an instant that you had not accepted my standard, but can't find out a why. Perhaps girls don't act according to reason or law. If so, I never can tell what they are liable to do I suppose. That isn't the problem however. The problem is to know how to please a girl whose system of symbols and ideals you don't know. Life is as much a puzzle too, I suppose; and only living will bring proof of the successes and failures. Best wishes to a friend who is highest.

Leslie

Alice met Leslie in college but in her second year he was already teaching in Ironwood. Evidently while at college they must have attended the same church or at least discussed that subject, as he refers to Sunday School Class and he refers to spiritual and philosophical questions in his letters. It seems that they were in similar majors, hers being Geography in Elementary Ed., and his being Social Studies for High School. Here's a short dissertation on the church he's going to in Ironwood. Excerpt from Oct. 7, 1928 letter.

... The following Sunday I went to church and have been going Sunday's since. I don't think the Methodist Episcopal Church here is very much except the Men's S.S. class. I have not heard a good sermon yet. On one occasion it was a harvest festival supreme in decoration and the preacher pro-tem gave an address on the fearful and revengeful God, thus tossing to the dust a glorious chance to give an illustrated lecture or sermon on the gracious and wondrous God.... [He gives a survey of his social life, which I imagine Alice will participate in when she gets to the Iron River area to teach.]

As teachers, we go out on week-end hikes. Sunday afternoons—- Say, we have a dandy time. None would miss, especially the girls from out of state once they can be coaxed to join the parties. We always have supper and get back by 9 o'clock in the evening.

I like the extra-curricular activity very much and am always going somewhere. My boys (in class) like me for that. But those pesty girls. I can't handle them as I should. If I could only grab them by the back of the neck like I can the boys, I could teach them a few things. I don't believe girls ever learn by talking to them.

Things are going wonderful for me in Ironwood now but the first two week-ends were so blue and lonesome I had to walk by myself. On my second Sunday here I have not a memory of where I walked except that it was out in Wis. somewhere. I went to the show too— but didn't know a thing about it after I got home.

We have half planned on coming to Marquette for Thanksgiving vacation but am not very sure of that. I may go deerhunting instead.

If I do go to Marquette, however, and you happened not to be gone somewhere else—I'll see you and tell you more about the time since our last meeting.

Your letter was such a nice letter that I made my mother read it. I also told her what type of a girl you were. I said you were so very good that it was difficult for you to make friends. That's not quite the truth, but just????something of the situation as I see it.

Remember when we returned from Sugar Loaf along the lake? Once I was tempted to kiss you but from sheer respect for your standards I refrained and now I feel that the fact that I didn't is proof that I liked you more than if I had.

I have no steady girl in Ironwood but I have not had a date yet either except the two from Iron Mountain. Then I made a date because the girl was from Illinois and was alone while I was somewhat known and had as good a chance as any of making the convention a happy occasion. With her, too, I accepted her standard. It was not yours—neither better nor worse—only hers—after the second evening she kissed me voluntarily as a token of appreciation for my friendship and efforts to see that she enjoyed herself.

This person is Mary Morrison—26 years old and a member of our hikes. She is not good looking, is short but has the ability to aid in many ways on the hike, etc. I'll send you a picture of her if I ever take one. Also will send you one of me if I get one worth the trouble—which isn't much.

There isn't much more news of a suitable humor to write. My troubles are plenty but they are packed on my back where neither I nor you know very much about them. Where they ride best; and where other folks can't add to them by unwanted sympathy. Will close with an apology for poor spelling and worse writing; but with best wishes.

A friend, Leslie

Dec. 21, 1928

Dear Friend,

I am sending you a Christmas letter because you are one of the few friends I really want to see. I wish I could get over to Marquette or Munising but I don't believe I will....

I have kept steady company with the same girl I told you about since last fall. Quite a record for me as I didn't do it at Normal. But then it is different now with less time to waste prospecting and with the good fortune of liking the first one....She is not of your kind exactly,...for you perhaps would trust me to take care of myself more than she. I'm an amateur admitted; but why tell me what I know. I can see that you are a trust of your very dear friend in Munising. [Owen] Tell him for me that he is a marvel in selecting a worthy cause.

Say, Alice, to me you are about the true meaning of Good Will. In my friendship with you, though disapproving my methods or ways of showing friendship a tiny bit, I have ever admired one of your qualities. "Never say anything if you can't say something good."... Being Irish and very fiery, I flash remarks that carry irony, contempt, and much sarcasm. I never mean a word of it....You perhaps never noticed it because of your still temperament. Usually with you I was calm, only a few times rising to emotional stages, and never very tense in oral conversation. I rested when with you...so great a change from every day life. It was something almost bordering on religion, in fact; much like going to a church to lie down daily cares. I didn't have to talk of them even; your soft voice; slow deliberative movements all spoke a language of re-assurance. I should like to be with you again some time and hope to, again.

I appreciate your letters very much Alice so don't forget to write....I wish to be thankful of your friendship. You seem to be a strong ship making eight knots on a direct course; I, a plane, with power to spare but with no target save a flash of a distant meteor.... Oh, for some real bearings again; and the nearest I come is at church and even there I often get dislodged by over-orthodox sermons.

Ever a friend who wishes you God Speed success in life.

Leslie O'B.

Feb. 9, 1929

Dear Alice

I received your wonderful letter yesterday and it really is "copy" from the highest source. The writing itself speaks neatness and thoroughness. It also speaks a lot in all that borders on Perfection....I showed it to another teacher to read....She marvelled at it very much and her comment was, "The girl sure writes religion and idealism into her letters without being conscious of the fact."...[much talk about their friendship and the friendship of the other girls in his life]...

In all I'm in good health and getting along as well as any semi-revolutionist in this quiet town. I'm all right but not quite settled down as to the whole meaning and purpose of life.

As ever, Leslie

March 13, 1929

Dear Sister,

I received your most inspiring letter to-day and was very much pleased with what you said. I am happy to think I could be nice to you. Last spring I had the privilege of liking you in my way; but showing self control as to showing it in my way. You believed that my symbolism was perhaps a little unjustified. Anyway, I determined to keep the friendship and adopt your symbols instead. That is why I never argued or quarreled. I kept your friendship by proving to you that you were the object of my liking———not my particular ways of displaying friendship.

The part that pleased me most was that you have agreed that there is some love between us which is of the noble, true, lasting kind——not a passion of the moment...but rather feared that after a few days you might think it mere sensuality.

As I think of the evening and the Sunday walk, I think of how much more free were my spirits because of your company....How much more free to call you Alice. Before I had called you that because Miss Halstead would have seemed so cold; though I feared that the intimacy of Alice might also bring your disapproval....

I only have seen Miss Morrison once since I came back. I told her of my wonderful time in Marquette. She accepts it well but is not overly happy about it. I told her about you too; so that no other teacher can tell her I...had another sweetheart....

I won't forget that I said I might be back again this spring and if I come you may be sure we have the walk. In fact I have about determined to come back.

Love from Brother Leslie

Nov. 27, 1929

Dear friend Alice,

As I was thinking over the many things I had to be thankful for, I reflected a while on our friendship. I wondered if you had decided that I was a broken bubble, a misplaced hope, an unworthy friend, and ungrateful boy. I hope you can still see in me a little more than ashes and dust and misery for really I am living and though not content; still enjoy myself at times for short periods.

As I sit here and look over the snapshots in my book I can relive our few nice trips in the woods together....As I think of it all I wonder if Mother Nature could talk if she could tell us what was wrong. We enjoyed those days with her and now we have come apart yet still living with Mother Nature....

A week ago, I took ten of my camera club boys out for a hike and we took pictures. When we came home I felt that I had been soothed by Nature even while trying to make ten others better acquainted with Nature. In fact I love nature, and now don't complain about cold weather but take advantage of a warm home, a nice ice rink, and wonderful snow clad hills to slide on....Hope you still think of me as a friend.

Leslie

P.S. If you don't answer I won't bother you again.

Jan. 10, 1931

Dear Friend Alice,

A Happy New Year from a friend to you. I hope you are as optimistic about the coming seasons as I am. I hope you had as pleasant a vacation as I did.

I haven't heard from you in a long time, and in the meantime I sometimes wonder how Alice is making it with the romance with the dear Mr. Tredway. It seems so fairytale-like in its scope. Understand—I have never breathed a word about it to anyone—- and never will tell anyone about it.

I wondered Christmas if you were as happy as I. In the two weeks vacation I spent about all the time with the girl of my choice—Mary Morrison— at her home and environs in Jamaica, Illinois....

In Ironwood I am getting along fine. My Supt. and Prin. have paid many compliments to my work this past year...

I'll get a lot of work in the woods next week, for I'll be out about every night gathering material for projects on Iroquois Indians with all the boys who want help in selecting willow, elm, ash and other woods or bark that they intend to work up in their project. We are going to make a whole Indian village to scale...I just know it is going to be lots of fun....

Will close, Leslie O'B

I found these letters interesting because it shows Alice's love for the psychological and spiritual nature of mankind. They also exhibit her high moral standards and honesty.

As you will see in the following letter, Alice is already listening to peoples woes!!

Feb. 8, 1931

Dear Alice,

It has been quite a while since I sat down to write you a letter, and I feel rather lonesome for the chance again...Today I like to write , because I'm feeling rather restless. I'm not at all satisfied with things, I feel something is the matter. Yet, I'm healthy and have been having a pretty good time. I just can't say what ails me but I know its a mental state of some kind....

I've tried all kinds of cures this week...I rested,...went to a wild party where some had too much too drink...I worked on my school projects and I was high strung all day....

Sat. nite I went to a dance...when I came out of the dance...I went for a walk...walked about 3 miles in the beautiful moonlight and glistening snow about 2 A.M. That made me very much improved.... Those 3 miles of walk were the best part of this week-end.

Today I thought I'd feel better if I were married but I don't know as any state would neutralize this except to get outside and walk it off...I 'll walk...to church...then I'll walk home again and go to bed....

I'm enclosing that picture I mentioned. Really I'm a bit fleshier than it portrays for I put on two pounds this week. Maybe I'm like a child with growing pains—developing into a man so fast it actually hurts....I'm on my way and would like to know where I'm bound for. Perhaps I'm in a forest or tunnel this week and will soon come out into the light again.

Well, as Lowell Thomas-Voice of the Air for the Literary Digest-says, "So Long until Tomorrow."

Best Wishes, Leslie

The last letter from Leslie was on a card with a picture of a lake on May 24, 1931. On the back it said,

A Token for Remembrance Sake

Suppose that the picture on reverse side were of Trout Lake. Look closely and you may see a young couple crouched under a boat to

secure shelter from the heavy hail and rain storm. If my eyesight is not failing me, the girl has black wavy hair and the boy light hair. E'en tho' their dinner is beyond reach, what care they? Two can live on Love while one would starve on it.

The family were very supportive during these two years. Alice was at college and teaching, away from home, and lonely. I also said I would talk more about Clara. These letters tell of Clara's years as she was finishing grammer school and moving to Munising to go to High School, a teen-ager in the 30's. They also tell of life on the farm in the letters from Grandma and George. Myrtles letters are about her big move to the farm in Rock, Michigan, which tell a little about life in the country in that time period.

Jan. 25, 1929

My dear sister Alice,

I received your letter but I did not get the knickers or waist. I got the letter on my birthday and was surprised not to get the knickers. All the kids in school are wearing or figuring on wearing their knickers and skiing down hill. I skiied a couple of times but I don't like to without knickers. I wish you would send them right away please.

Well, we're having a vacation this week, but we'll have to go a week more next spring....Mr. Mall's got some cooking utensils, a heater stove with lids on for a stove, a lamp with a glass about an inch thick, a dishpan and other things at the schoolhouse. HaHa. I hope he can get the place fixed up so we can get to school this year. Oh "Shoot" I'll be glad when I get out of this Limestone school....

Mother and I went loggin' today. Boy!! the snow is deep, clear above my waist. It's fun loggin' but lots of work. We sawed five logs this morning and "broke" a road. Carley skidded them this afternoon to the loading place. I went with Carley to Traunik and [got] a load of logs Saturday....

Say, haven't we been having some terrible weather this month? It was twenty below one morning and fifteen below three mornings or more, and I don't mean Centigrade either. Ha Ha.

Dad has been pretty sick, he never got entirely over the flu. Well Alice I'll have to get some wood for the night———

Adios, "B. R." Clara

Clara's middle name is Ruth and she's one of the younger children in the family, hence the nickname Babe Ruth.

Sat. 26, 1929

Well, I didn't mail this letter yet so will write some more....

Say! What other subjects are you takin besides Sociology, Latin and Teaching? We skipped nearly all constructions in Geometry and jumped into Book II. I had exams in Geometry. I got 92%. He wouldn't give me an A. I left out three words on one Theorem that I proved and he took off five points. Well that gave me a 95%. He was "bound" I wasn't going to get an A so he took three points off for no reason at all so's to make it below 93%. If he don't give me an A in Geometry on my report he's "gonna" get his head knocked off "Begorie".

I've still got the musical instrument [an accordian?] and can play most anything on it. "Among my Souveniers," "Blue Heaven," "Massa in de cold Ground," "Prisoners Song," and others I haven't got room for...Well,

Adios again.

Gertrude is Myrtle (Mother's sister's) daughter and is writing Alice a thank-you letter. Mother was very generous and probably really enjoyed having her own money she earned from teaching.

217 W. Division Street
Ishpeming, Michigan

January 23, 1930

Dear Aunt Alice,

Here I am at home. I just got done with the dishes and it being Friday I didn't have anything to do so I thought I would write you a letter....

Gee! Guess what I got on my examinations. I got A+ in History, A in Arithmetic, A in English, B in Geography, B in Spelling, and I think I got an A in Literature....

Gee! I am taking music lessons now and it sure does keep me busy if I do say so. I have to come home from school and practice my music lessons and after supper I have to do my school work until nine o'clock and some times 'til ten. "Alice", I have a new piece called "The World is Waiting for the Sunrise." Gee! It sure is a beautiful piece....

Baby [her brother Bob] has been sick all week. You know I take care of him for a nickel every nite after school and it was my turn this week...I have or will have after tomorrow, sixty three cents. I am keeping my money for a pair of "Roller Skates" because they are on sale this month and next.

"Alice," Gee! you were a dear to send me that goods for my dress. Oh! Boy! If my dress don't look beautiful. I will thank you for it when you come over because I don't know how else to thank you...
Your loving niece,

Gertrude

March 5, 1930

Dearest Sister Alice,

...I suppose you must have gotten George's letter by now, saying he was home? I was home to see him Friday night, Saturday and Sunday. Mrs. Ford and Mother came after me and Fred J., George and Evelyn brought me back.... [Evelyn is Tom's (Mother's brother) daughter]....If you want to see him, you'll have to go home "pronto"

because he is going back as soon as he gets a letter from the school. I made he, Fred, and Evelyn promise to come to the "tourney" here Saturday night. I sure hope they don't break their promise....

Gee I had a "heap good time" during the week-end even though it did storm all the while. I got home about 6:30 Friday night. Saturday I got up at 6:30 and worked steady on Dad's books til 12:30. Some work believe me. If you make a mistake of one cent, the whole books are wrong and won't balance...[that night] I stayed with Evelyn and talked, worked arithmetic and looked at pictures etc...Oh say Sis, have you got a big enough bed to keep two partners during two nights of the Marquette "tourney" ?...

Write right away, Sister.
Clara Halstead

(l-r) George, Alice, and Clara were close in age and friendship. This photo taken around 1921.

1009 North Pine
Marquette, Mich.

March 19, 1930

My Dear Sister,

How's the girl?...

I went to see Clara last Saturday, I thought maybe she would like to come home but she was in Marquette to see the basketball tournament....

I'm still cutting poles. Its tough cutting when one hasn't nothing to walk on. James has gone to see about getting the Eckerman forty. I hope he gets it.

How's school? Still what it used to be? I've 23 trees tapped, but no sap yet. [Maple trees for syrup.] Too cold I guess. Maybe I'll have some maple candy by the time you come home again. I can't think of any more to tell you , only the roads is good....Write soon,

Your Brother

Lovingly, George

April 13, 1930

My dearest Sister Alice,

Such!! is life. Nowhere to sleep and to eat. Of course I won't starve but, O Boy!! You can keep your wonderful town of Munising, for all me!....

Mrs. Russat was sure nice to let me stay. there, but what'll I do?...I have just five cents to my name....

What I am writing this letter for, is to ask you to ask Mr Tredway if I can clean his house up...and tell him to tell me I can. I'll promise I'll do the very best I can, going over the entire house, even in the basement if he wants me to....I don't know what's going to happen to me, but it'll turn out alright in the end.

Well, hoping to hear from you and also Mr Tredway

Goodbye, Clara

April 24, 1930
My dear Sister,

I got your letter to-day,...I think you are right about all. Now I have a nice place to stay, I think. Not to work tho!! I am paying five or seven dollars a week. I think it is five tho. At the home of Mrs Beaupry. I both eat and sleep there. She is real nice to me....

I have a nice big room all by myself. The nicest room I've ever had with a big double bed....I am staying with Mrs. Peterson's son tonight. I get 50 cents for it. I wish I could do it every night. I wouldn't go in the "hole" then...Goodbye,

Love, Clara

Clara in high school

Clara was an early women's lib proponent as you can see in the following letter. I think I modeled after her.

June 10, 1930

My dearest Sister,

Well Sis' our school days for my Junior year are soon over. I've just begun to like Munising now, since it's ...summer...and I naturally have to leave. Here's hoping I get a good job for next year so I can come back here again....No housework for me anymore....I'd rather dress as a boy and ride tractor, split or saw wood, shovel snow, or nearly anything if I could, than to work for any more women doing housework....

We went on our class picnic to Indian Lake and the Big Springs Saturday. I had our car. We surely had a peach of a time. I had the car all decorated with red and white streamers, and we wore white sweaters, white sailor pants and a red and white tam, or rather jockey cap....

I am as Ever, Your friend, Clara

The work George refers to is probably working for the Gov't, either State or Federal, putting out a forest fire in their area. Remember this is during the Great Depression and work was hard to come by.

R.R.2
Iron River, Michigan
%Mrs Olaf Cristenson

Sept. 8, 1930

Dear sister Alice,

Hows the teacher? How many kids do you have to whip an hour? It gets kind of tiresome on the arms don't it? I invented a special machine that takes all the work out of whipping the kids. It only costs five dollars a month as long as it lasts. But, no kidding, how are you getting along? No ornery kids I hope....

I've been working pretty steady since I came home. I worked 108 hours at the fire in 5 days. Its out now though....We lost the hay we had over to Shaw's place. It burned with the fire....

Well Alice , if you don't write don't blame me for not writing.

Lovingly yours,

Your Brother, George

Sept. 14, 1930

My dear daughter Alice

I was so glad to get your letter and to hear that you had such a nice homey place to board. I hope you will continue to like it there next May as well as you do now. Also hope you enjoy your school even better but I am sure you will when you get acquainted with all those little ones. I guess Angela has an increase in the number of pupils in her school this term. [Limestone one- room grammer school?]

Jack [Alice's youngest brother] is going and two next door and three or four Kentuckians, all boys. There surely are a bunch of boys in that school. Jack likes to go to school, he says.

Well we got home from the plains last Aug. 30th, two weeks ago yesterday. When we got to Seney, we got a telephone that forest fires were all around the place, so we came home as fast as possible. We called at Mr. Tredway's to see you and you were gone. I was sorry because Iron River is a long ways off. I suppose George told you about Shaw's barn burning hay and all.

The boys have had pretty steady work since they came home. They worked night and day for a while at the fire. Then, after the election they went to work at the dyke they are building at Trout Lake. They have been with a truck hauling steel from Chatham…I mean steel rails. An Ishpeming company is building it. The big steam dipper went by the other day. I didn't see how they could get through the Trout Lake road but they made it all right.

I haven't seen Clara since Labor Day. George, though, saw her in Chatham Friday. She was at the Fair. Too bad she didn't strike work of some kind. Hope she does soon.

Well Alice, did you vote? Well the Senator and Governor and nearly all the rest I voted for got the nomination.

Write and let me know all about your school when you get time. Don't work too hard, keep your nerves in hand, take all your troubles as a joke and laugh it off....Don't take little grievances too seriously, they are only children and don't mean all they do and say. So let it all roll off like water off a ducks back. Well, goodbye Alice, I must start supper from

Mother

I have four dinners to put up every morning. You know what that means...baking.

Oct. 2, 1930

Dearest Sister Alice,

...I have had six teeth filled and have one more to get filled...I took a bite of apple before dinner. Well that was the end. Talk about ache!!!!! O! O! I couldn't eat any dinner...It doesn't only hurt but it is going to cost me $16. I am going to be thru Friday night thank goodness!! He will fill the last one and clean and polish them all.

I start working at the A & P store to-night after school. I won't get much, it will take four weeks or more to pay the dentist and five or six to buy me a new coat....I don't know whether to draw my $20 from the bank and pay Dr. Ruggles, or let him wait 'til I make that much money....

We have the day off tomorrow on account of Teachers Institute. I am going to clean Mr. Tredway's house up for him. All the kids are going on a hike but I'm going to work. Ambitious I'd say....

How are you getting along in school now?...How's all the kids? Hope you have by now overcome your lonesomeness....

Yours Sincerely, Clara

Oct.16,1930

My dear daughter Alice,

Well, how are all those little kids? Lets hope they all get A in deportment this month. Hope your boys have all turned good and make a chum of their teacher.

The boys are working nights at the Dyke. The first part of the month it was nice and warm and moonlight. But now its dark and wet weather. So of course they sleep daytimes. I didn't have breakfast quite ready when they got home this morning as they got here a little earlier than usual so James went right to bed.

Mrs. D. was in Munising Tuesday and she saw Clara at the A & P store. She said she was getting on fine and liked her work. Myrtle was here the last two Sundays. I am glad we are having such nice weather so long so she can make the trip. I'll be sorry when she can't come. Jack and Charlie are in school to-day. Jack is getting so he can read his book first rate, and likes to go to school....George got a bad sprain on his ankle but he had Saturday and Sunday night to rest up in so he didn't lose any time. Hope you are well and enjoying your work....Well good luck Alice & good night from

Mother

Nov. 7, 1930

Dearest Sister Alice,

Was I surprised to get an answer so soon!!! Here's hoping I get another one as quickly!!....

I'm going to ask one of the kids to take me home Sunday. I can't help but get so lonesome for George and Mother that I can't help it....

You said you might…get me my ring. We have to get them next week, and I'm busted, having paid the balance of my bill to Ruggles [the dentist]....If you could help me to get it maybe I could pay you back after awhile, if you wanted me to.

George sent me a ten dollar bill, but I put that in his bank account for him. If you are planning to get my ring, I'll have to get it right away. You know, I never knew that Mr. Tredway took you to Iron River 'til last week when, because I was feeling kinda sick and my eyes were sore, I went over there to lie down for awhile....Listen here, you have to come home for Xmas....I'd like to go home Thanksgiving if I can possibly get off at the store....

Cum amore, Clara

Dec. 6, 1930

Dear daughter Alice:

I had a letter from Myrtle and was so sorry to hear that you were too sick to go and see her but hope that you are entirely well by this time....

Are you going to put on a program for Christmas? Hope your health is good enough to stand the strain. I suppose you've got it all figured out but hope it isn't a very long tiresome one.

Clara was here for Thanksgiving dinner and went home again Sunday afternoon...

The boys are still working at the Dyke. Well the bus came before I finished this letter so I'll have to send it out tomorrow. Hoping this finds you feeling fine and expecting to see you soon.

From your loving Mother.

March 29, 1931

My Dear Sister,

Well, here is some good news. We are moving to that darling little farm next month, about three or four weeks from now. We have paid some on it and we are to get most of the money for our shop tomorrow. The man who is buying our shop takes the business over Wednesday the 1st. Mac is going to teach him how to repair tires and handle the machinery. Our rent is all paid for the rest of the time we are to be here. We paid $60.00 yesterday for that. Gee!!!!!! Sis, come Thursday nite we will go see Mrs. M and I'll tell you about our place. Mac is sure enthusiastic about it . He said after the lady consented to give it to us at our price cash, he could have hugged all the cows!!!

Everything is ideal. Mac wants to take you down but I say wait, we will only be 24 miles from Escanaba and we can meet you there and you can come up after we move. There are some roosters in the coop which we shall have a chicken dinner from. We don't believe in having or feeding anything that does not produce. We will be closer from Munising than we are now via the way of Little Lake. It is just 16 miles from Little Lake so Mr. Tredway can bring Clara up just the same. You can even have a bath in a real bath tub there too. Gee!!! Alice, I wish were were there for Easter so you could see it. You will never want to leave in the summertime. The most beautiful orchard, lawn swing. Will look for you Thursday nite. By, by, lots of love,

from Myrtle

April 10, 1931

Dearest Sister Alice,

I got your letter last week....I'm writing right back, but if you don't get it right away, you can know that it was because I didn't have a two cent stamp until payday....

Gee! I wish this was my last of four years of College instead of High School. I wish I knew what I really want to take up. I had always wanted secretarial work, and now, it would be unbearable to be pinned up in an office, especially me, because as much as I love the woods and the out-of -doors, it's not probable that I could be shut in, in an office, that is like a prison for me....What do I want to be? If I'd had more science, I'd be a nurse, maybe, 'cause now I'd like to be, that is, a welfare nurse, if I'd had more Mathematics. But no, a little of everything, and too much commercial...I'm so undecided.

Were you home for Easter? I worked during the whole vacation at the store so I couldn't go home...[I believe she still worked at the A&P grocery on Elm Street.]

I'll have to get to work and study Latin so I'd better ring off for now. When is Mr. Tredway coming home?

S'long and Good luck,

Your Sister, Clara

April 12, 1931

My Dear Sister,

I suppose you are real tired this morning after the play. Hope everything was a big success both financially and playwrite.

I am writing to tell you we are moving a week from today. The lady is moving out as she is sick and we must take care of our stock and start to farm. They all tell us we are going to be very late. We will have some help so we can get along fine. The chickens are producing just fine now. We were down there Wednesday and yesterday. We can see the kind of soil we have best now. All muck down on the lower land and clay and sandy loam on the higher land, so I guess we have about the best. We were to a big auction sale yesterday and met a lot of our neighbors....Gee, I believe we are going to like it....

Myrtle

Rock, MI.

April 30, 1931

My Dear Sister,

Was sure glad to get your letter. Well as usual there is so much to tell about it is hard to start.

About school, Gertrude has high school teachers and she is in the assembly. Vivian is in a room where they have both the 5th and 6th grade, some change for her. And Dorothy is home with the mumps.

Mac sure is some farmer. So far this week he has plowed, roller disked and harrowed eight acres of land. The neighbors say they never saw a farmer do so much. He milks two cows night and morning and I milk one and Gert and Vivian each milk one. The girls can milk real good and so can Mac. It only takes us about forty five minutes in the barn and the separator. I don't go down to the milk room at all when I finish my cow. I come in it is about fifteen to seven. I dress the two boys and prepare breakfast while Mac runs the separator and feed the calves....I fix the girls lunches and start my work....Today I washed. I had a big bag of clothes for Mother along with my washing.

We drove down late Sunday afternoon....We were exactly 26 miles from the farm. They are moving up to the old place. Mother was whitewashing [the log cabin] and her eye was badly burned. Dad, as usual was in a terrible "sweat". Mother says she don't see what his hurry is, he only hollers and she would rather he would stay where they are so when she is working she can't hear him!!

Mother wants me to put in an acre of asparagus. She says she will give me the plants. Gee, Al, it is beautiful here today. I am getting up my curtains....Hope you can come down soon....Did you say you would be finished the 5th of June? The children are through two weeks from to-morrow....

Your Sis, Myrtle

Rock, MI.

May 7, 1931

My Dear Sister,

Well Al, this is the first rainy day....so I'll drop you a line.

Did I tell you the folks split the two forties for George and James? They are going into chickens. I guess they are doing a lot of work plowing and they bought and tore down and hauled Linberg's camp up for lumber to build with.

Gee! Al—I wish you had come up last Sunday. Waited all day for company and no one came. Had cakes, two dressed roosters and salad. And our house looked lovely all fixed up. Well we have the barn work down to 30 minutes now, not so bad?

I believe I forgot to tell you the most important thing about Vivian's grade. In the morning they say a blessing when school first opens and at the close of school they all repeat the Lord's Prayer. Dorothy is getting along just fine. Viv says she gets all 100's and her teacher cannot understand her low marks. Junior said if I would give him a piece of cake he would keep quiet but he discovered he didn't like the raisins so he isn't keeping his promise. Gertrude stirred up a spice cake last night....while I made a couple of custard pies.

Mac has finished hauling out all the manure onto his field. All he has to do now is drag and seed. Then we must finish our potato ground, it is nearly all ploughed. We are using new ground.

...Mac and I are going to take a look at the woods where they cut wood after the children come home from school....Mac is using this time to get feed ground up for the cows. He ground a barrel that doesn't last six cows very long.

Oh yes, by the way Mac says he might have to call on you yet to assist him financially for a short time. He has $400 coming for supplies within three months...but we may have to pay the balance of $300 before that time. That amount is to be paid when she secures a clear deed...The meeting of court is to be held the 11th of May.... We paid every cent we got from the shop. Then Mac collected some bills and we paid $35 to move down here and we have enough money to do all our spring work. I have the cream checks we received since we came here still untouched. Now don't start to think about this, we *may not need it at all....I'm telling you so you won't go out and buy us any Birthday present, and I want you to pay your debt.*

...You don't need to worry about shipping your things, the last of school. I'll come up after you that day and our car can surely take all your belongings...Some time later, if you want them in Munising, we can take them up...Lots of love,

Your Sister, Myrtle

Wednesday in May

My Dear Sister,

Well we arrived here O.K, 5:10 in the morning. That sure was some storm trailed us all the way back. The children were some frightened, so they informed us.

Oh! Yes, Al, Mac said if it was convenient you could send the check right along as he will need it the first part of next week. And we will try and get it back to you as soon as possible. Gee! This sure saves us a lot. We would have to go to Ishpeming and get some one on a note if you didn't do this for us. We assure you we appreciate it very much. And if praying helps, you may get your wish. May God keep you and bless you.

Your Sis, Myrtle

May 25, 1931

Our Dearest Sister,

I am in receipt of both of your dear letters and must thank you greatly for the loan. I assure you Mac can make it now. I am in great hope that nothing will occur to cause you to regret lending it to us.... We were home yesterday and learned that Mother and Mr. Tredway had quite a bit of trouble getting back. They didn't get to the farm until 10 o'clock right time, that was 11 o'clock his time. The wire broke off from the battery and they were stuck about 2 miles this side of the state road for about 1 and 1/2 hours. Then someone came along and make a connection with a screwdriver for him and they got on the state road about 2 miles this side of Trenary. Then they stopped again for about an hour, then Oscar, Mr. Tredway's clerk came along and after breaking the tow rope about 20 times they finally arrived at Trenary, where they waited over an hour for the car to be repaired.

Oh! yes Al, I must tell you we have a new baby in our family. We call her May because she was born, Thursday night in May. She seems real healthy as her Mother is about the best cow in the herd. Well when we found out she was going to calve, out came the agriculture book. We found she must have a box stall so Mac made a nice one for her and we filled it with straw and she still has her calf with her, as per the agriculture book, but tomorrow she must leave her baby and go out to pasture. We have left her on the good meadow since she was sick. [Pregnant?]

Well Alice, you should have been with us today, we spent the day in the woods . We cut wood and we all had a good time too. We all went in the Ford truck, seemed like old days when Pa used to come up to Gwinn after us. We cut and hauled quite a bit of wood about 3 cords....I guess then we cut it all with the sawing machine. Sure went slick and didn't take much time either....

Well Al, it is ten, that is late for a farmer, especially after being out in the woods all day, so Nite Nite. Lots of love and best wishes for your happiness.

Myrtle

[Notes below that were on the top of the page. I think Myrtle is referring to Alice marrying Owen.]

If it is God's will may your wish be granted.—Thank you again—"Thine will be done on earth as it is in heaven."

Motherhood

MOTHER STARTED this journal July 20, 1933. Keep in mind that this is very personal and though I've tried to edit the journal of excess rambling and the mention of people outside the immediate family circle as I knew it, what I kept is what interested me. I tried to focus on her spirituality, her relationship with my father, her daily life and stuff that seemed historical politically. Her relationship with her two children was a major theme and so I kept the passages where we were her focus. Sometimes it may seem that she was more favorable in her response to me, her second child, but I put that down to her being more comfortable the second time around. I certainly never felt favored as I grew up in this home.

July 20—Have had a dreadful time trying to keep up a diary in the regular form. It will seem much nicer to write just when I please, as much as I care to say with no limitation of space.

Today has been a regular day, one to make any housewife happy and tired. Owen literally pulled me out shortly after seven. Since then—ironing few dresses I can wear, making waste basket for orchid room, looking over six quarts of blueberries, canning them a new way (with rhubarb), mulching in the garden, a trip to Belfry's [Meat Market], dinner, and looking over eight quarts of raspberries. Owen, the dear, helped as long as he dared, it being "payday"... [At the store.]

July 23—...Today was rather an unusual Sabbath. No church and no S.S. Just about to eat lunch and Dr. and Mrs. Grawn (the first Dr. of M. [Medicine or Munising?] who had his office in the back of Owen's first drug store of the town) dropped in on their way to lower Mich. While they were looking at the store, Mother, Mrs. D. and Clara called. At about five o'clock we took to a woodsey road about five miles long. At its end we hiked back....The evening was usual—"Time" and "Golden Books", 'Tillylass Scandal', by Barrie, music good over the radio and onion-lemon tea-sandwich supper in the kitchen. [Sunday evenings my father read books out loud. Brynhild and perhaps others came to listen.]

Owen and Alice made a trip to Florida the previous winter, for their honeymoon. Alice, always interested in geography and flora and fauna, wrote a book covering their trip. This will be referred to frequently in this journal as she tries to put that book together. The baby she refers to is my sister Janis.

July 29—Writing up Tarpon Golf Course [for her book]-Owen is ever dear and kind to me....Canning raspberries and eating raspberry pie. Very obliging young man, Rowan, brings them to me each day. Soon it will be cherries for the tree is loaded. Should like to know where to go to have my baby-or who to have if I stay with Owen....[Home birth?]

Aug. 2, 1933—Just returned from Dr. Gageby's office-I must go to the hospital [to have her baby.] Well, it could be much worse. Have felt dreadful today....

Aug. 12—Some secrets of our happiness. My dear one never fails to tell me when something is good. Tonight-rare roast beef etc.-blackberry pie. "This is good eating, Alice. Beans, potatoes, and meat tastes good." Who wouldn't find joy-even tho' it caused pain to bend to oven so often-in making a big dinner...Weight and pains bothered me today....I wish I weren't so big and clumsey these summer days.

Aug. 21—It was just a year ago today that Owen came to Rock [Myrtles] for dinner, that we went out for a ride in the woods and Owen decided once and for all time that I would be the one to make him happy the rest of his life, God willing. It took me hours to go to sleep up in the loft bed with Myrtle, (they were hours filled with happy dreams) for he had my bed.

Aug. 25—Friday 4:30 am-The time has come! It feels like I am entering a very black night. But I do not fear; for I have prayed and feel that God is very near at hand. But I do dread it. There is one consolation-it will soon be over. I have quite made up my mind that it will be a boy. I do not mind. He will bear the name of Tredway—and—it will be my greatest pleasure to make him worthy of it. If I can teach him hon-

Owen and Alice at time of marriage.

esty, self respect, respect for others-then—I shall teach him of God's goodness and beauty by studying the wild life in the forest-the flowers—and man.

I have pains that are very nearly like my monthly pains. Everything is in order. I would have cleaned the house today but it can wait. I enter this new experience with faith in God....

September—(Written last part of month)...Went to hospital at 7:30am before breakfast. Owen took me over in the car (Buick). A nurse undressed me, put me to bed, made me ready for the doctor's examination. Dr. came. Examined me, and explained what was happening. All was going well... After noon...I grew so tired with the pains that I was nearly under when they called the Dr. I can remember his pleasant voice as he called to me "Mrs. Tredway, your baby is ready to come. Bear down, a little more." He was not there when I woke to hear the girls call to me "You have a fine baby girl. are you glad?" I could only answer "No, because now I'll have to have another, to have a boy." I had really wished for a girl. The next day, Mother and George called....

I was to come home, Sept. 6, Owen's birthday, but felt much too poorly.

At home. Had capable Ann Knaus to do work and care for babe. Stayed in bed mornings—lay by fireside pms and nites. Did not lift baby or carry her for nearly two weeks. Got worse till Dr. fixed me up....

Doing my own work fifth week.

After this Mother goes into a dissertation of how the women of Munising and the Methodist Episcopal Church, which they belong to, are so aloof to her, and that they lack of acceptance of the May-September marriage. She fantasizes how she'll fix the house up and get all the proper service to entertain them at some later time and ends with—

And what does it all matter if things are clean and comfortable and we are happy without all this. Besides I have dear small Janis and the flowers to watch grow—Real friends to write to, some to see-a multitude of other things to look forward to-maybe I can teach the S. S. class. Those darling girls how they've changed since that first summer when they all talk at once. Now they call after S. S. to chat an hour by the fireplace. God keep them and guide them.

Oct. 3—Took papa home today. Poor Mother will not only have to dig potatoes all day, but will have to nurse him all night. I know him, when she's around. Could never understand until now—I'd do even more for my loved one.

Oct. 8—Dull Sunday. Snaps of baby in bedroom.

Oct. 9—Baby's first smile. Was it an accidental twitch of the mouth? Charming letter from Ann Christensen. She's making a rock-garden to hide temper—or wear it out.... Bub making cottage. I wonder if he thinks of the autumn days we rode together in the 'open air' Ford? [I think Bub might be another of her beaux. Janis says he was a son of the Christensens, where she boarded in Stambough, that she liked a lot.] And what he thinks of me for marrying as I did. He expected it, I know. Should like to write to Albert. Both nice boys—for somebody. At least they're too good to remain bachelors.

Oct. 10—An enlightening smile again, from that sweet one, when I change her.

Oct. 11—And again. Today she talked back and squealed. Tried to get a snap but she wouldn't pose...

Oct. 18—I have had many pangs of remorse and regret today—Refused Clara a very small favor that wouldn't have hurt me the least but to grant-to take Papa out home so she could stay to see O—[Ole, who she married.] I did it because I feared dear Owen wouldn't like it. Did go to Rock. That to please his mood-and my craving. They [Myrtle and family] had a good time spoiling Baby. Girls made big fuss; Bob cute.

Oct. 24—...Janis (nearly five months) reaches—timidly—for rattle, shakes it—not timidly—violently. Laughs aloud. Had a bad day—knows cod liver oil by the glass [and wouldn't take it?]—liked tomato juice. Put sister [Janis says this is Ella, Owens's older sister] on a schedule tomorrow. She seems not to want to get up early. Has been late—a little every morn for breakfast—we are getting along nicely—no breaks. She is to get breakfast next week. There is much to do and I seem not to be able to get it done—will try harder.

Aunt Ella and Janis

Jan. 31, 1934—...Heard Roosevelt last night. The country is certainly making a fuss over him. I am sorry for him because of the magnitude of his task in which he must succeed. The "Time" [magazine] is all I seem able to read.

Feb.26—Meant to write yesterday but today serves as well. Yesterday the baby was six months old. Tomorrow we will have been married 18 months....

Owen—his same dear self. We could live together eternally and be happy—alone with God and Babe.

Sister[Ella]—working on a quilt for Janis. She likes to please....Our most important rift is radio. I like Stokowski and others-Boston Sym.—Met.—Philharmonic—She likes senseless drama-yet she always says how she likes good music. Does her share of work well.

Me—In love with babe and Owen—not unhappy with Sis—Working, working—not getting done what I'd like. Snowflake Quilt-story-photo album, scrap book, reading, baby, music, cleaning, cooking, visiting...must nurse babe now.

Mar.23—Babe is seven months on 25th ...

April 16-Tomorrow's program-if God Wills.
6:30-Baby
7:00-7:30- Wash and clean cupboards in bathroom
7:45-Bathe babe-make bed-baby cod liver oil
8:00-Breakfast-feed baby
8:30-Clean-bathroom
11:30-Wash and change
12:00-Work on map [for correspondance course]
12-30-Lunch
1:00-Baby
2:00-? Story? Babe for ride and shopping?
3:30-Babe to bed-rest-Write on story or shopping.
5:00-Care of Baby-Supper-dishes
7:30-Story
8:00? Visit-story?-sewing-and radio?

Dear, oh, dear, I'm as deeply mired as ever. There is so much to be done and nothing gets done!...

Sister [Ella] is leaving us Thursday.

April 19—Such a hollow unhappy feeling. Any other afternoon I'd be happy to be alone—but since I know she is gone I can hardly stand it. There is a lump in my throat which I can not care away. Sister really did help a lot by doing dishes after the meal she prepared each day.

April 21—How rich we are, dear God. The three of us well and in love with each other—with God's blessing on our home. Why should we scold because we can't have new electric range, new curtains, new refrigerator! Oh, that God will still reign on earth as well as in Heaven and help guide the leaders of this country thru the paths of righteousness-that He will bring justice to all-those who wrong (and forgive them) and those who suffer wrong. God, wilt thou always be my, Owen's, and Janis too, guide-and I thank thee.

May 2, 1934—Nearly a week of gorgeous weather-we're already in need of rain. Soon the bathroom and kitchen will be sparkling clean and there will be a fine refrigerator to gaze upon as well as to use....Owen rented A&P store building to Aanderud at forty [dollars?]—should help a little. Not getting my story finished.

June 15—...Vivian [sister Myrtles daughter] and Charlie [brother] have been here more than a week....If Helen comes I'll be going to school. That means more work. It will be nice—save the running back and forth. Janis has grown up a lot. Afraid of a dog today. Clings to me. She can get up to a sitting position alone. Has two teeth...at nine months. Creeps a little-like flying-backwards and forwards....

June 23—Day after tomorrow school starts. I'm all excited. Mrs. Barnes stopped to say she'd take baby for the summer if Peter were willing....

I would conjecture here that Owen has encouraged Alice to get her permanent teaching certificate, in case something happens to him. In order to do that, she needs to take continuing classes so she goes to Marquette to summer school. In those days people didn't commute fifty miles a day, so she stayed up there during the week.

June 27—Here at Bennet's in Marquette. A clean bunch they are Dr., Mrs., Ruth, George, Art, Davy, Matthew—and Rose. At school I have…McGowan and evolution can not fill in gaps with fact but will not fill it in with Biblical history….A letter from Owen thrilled me.

July 10—…Tomorrow music practice-study and prepare evolution chart-read geography references. I hope I get in the swing soon.

July 31, 1934—Tomorrow is commencement for me and I'm just as thankful to God, as that High School commencement in 1927-when my one prayer was that I would be. [Graduated?]

Aug. 22—…The Barnes are so indifferent. She hasn't been over tho she had my baby for six weeks this summer. The baby just screamed and took on over there. Everything strange….How sorry I am for Clara. She married, nothing to buy things with and how much one needs….

Oct. 18—…Registered college—such a happy feeling just to be there in the halls seeing familiar faces. Now I must get down to work. George enrolled in correspondance course, too. Father disappointed. I sorry I didn't see him in hospital.

[After a long dissertation on Janis and joys of motherhood, Alice continues], I guess I'm a born mother—I'm longing for another baby. If only Owen weren't so old. Then of course, there are the three months at beginning and end which are not too nice but they are soon forgotten when the dear one comes. I think I'd really try again if we had a first class obstetrician. How I'd like a boy.-and Owen would too if he only knew it.

Nov.15—Two great loads off my mind. Owen has arranged at last that Janis and I at least have an income after he is gone—was leaving it all to Marie [Owen's niece] save the house and a trust fund for Janis. It was very hard not to feel bitter about it. He has done enough for her already. And Marie is not coming up. I shall not feel kindly toward her until she apologizes- at least shows it in her manner—how ugly she has been toward me. ever since that fateful visit of hers with Mrs. Y. When she does, I shall be happy.

Vandenberg and Fitzgerald elected, Senator and Govenor.

Jan. 8, 1935—Menasha Hotel, Menasha, Wisconsin-I can shut all my worries out tonight and thank God I am here with Owen and Janis love, safe and sound. We are on our second day south to Florida. Baby walked and walked and walked today-holding my hand.

They have arrived in Florida and have rented a small house in Clearwater.

Jan 28—Janis walked today-she explored the house and the yard. We know now that tomorrow she will walk again—perhaps use her arms less in balancing. She has a great love for books and....She picks outs objects she knows...None are too minute to miss her eye....One great change has taken place. She just loves strangers...to make a fuss over her.

I wrote to Leslie and find he is in the CCC too, with a Master of Science in History-in the instructors role.

Feb.6, 1935—...Tasted my first of the Avocado pear—rather liked it—dark green-hardskinned egg shape-with hard seed which comes right out (size of pullet's eggs). We ate the soft tasty meat out with a spoon. They are about the size of very large lemons....Each day we have gone to the beach-Janis walks with Daddy on the beach and sees all the bow-wows.

Feb. 23—We have struck up an agreement with the Higbees [These were friends from Marquette that also went to Florida. Remember he was mother's Sunday School teacher] that they keep baby while we golf and we take them with us where we go in the car. I am keeping a record of services rendered and received as it is often very difficult to judge when there is no definite understanding....Owen's hair is the prettiest I've seen it. We've done a great deal of brushing. Too slow with my studies-must get one off Monday.

Daddy and Janis in Florida

March 5—We will never have Janis any sweeter. It is just a delight from her first "Peek", or "Bemare and Daddy" or "shoes and socks" or "got up" until her last "D'night" at seven. She behaves most beautifully when we have her out tonight at the Gray Moss Inn with the Higbee. She ate with the rest of us, my fish, b. potato, and beets, and tomatoes.

March 9—To the beach-work on Montaigne....

March 16—... Twenty six essays in this lesson-must write on friendship.

April 8—Played golf today with Daddy at Clearwater. Haven't been scoring lately. It is more enjoyable when we don't....

April 20—To Fishers tomorrow-and of course to church. The Higbees are getting ready to go, in fact they've moved out of their house into the Grey Moss Inn.

April 30—Here we are on our way home—248 miles. Cherokee Hotel-$2.50 dinner—room with bath and two beds. Green Cove Springs-We walked down to see the 40 foot spring (300 gal/min of 78 degree water all year round;) also the St John's river...[From here they took an extended trip up the east coast. South Carolina, Virginia and Washington DC.]

Passed near Monticello but missed it because of rain and cold....White House—Only a few rooms open—I loved the beautiful chandeliers. Pan American Building-Garden of commercial plants many of which I know from studies and Florida; its lovely Mexican and Indian designing and architecture. Most beautiful Printing—U.S. 2 cents stamps $1 bill—poor guide-woman—gossipy. Capitol: Hall of Flags, Hall of States, Congress in Session (disgusting it was to see the inattentive few there in each place—splendid guide—saw Congressional Library—The beauty of them all-Smithsonian Institute....

We continued on thru Ohio and into Michigan and at Otsego...inquired the whereabouts of the Bartons. [Emelines family?] They kept us there all night and fed us well. Uncle James [not Alices brother] told the story of the Romans and many others. Ellen was a bit cold that night but was pleasant in the morning. I loved her little wee lambs but they wouldn't let me hold them. She sent asparagus to Marie. I prayed and had faith that there would be only love between Marie and myself. We did have a pleasant visit and found her to be happier than usual. The children I love and always have.

May 13—We finished our trip today-2345 miles-14 days-only four of which were perfect. They were the first three and Sat. we stayed over in Casnovia. But we were grateful to the Hand that guided us safely back to our home without injury or even car trouble or tire trouble. At Casnovia, Sister [Ella, daddy's sister] was all upset when Marie[Ella's daughter] and children drove up at 7:00 AM. She'd tried very hard to make our visit pleasant,. which it was. Sour milk cakes, sausage, doughnuts one morning all was fine....We worked out Owen's family tree....Sister had plenty for Owen to do. He fixed a lock-hired the cellar wall set up, helped change a bed....I hardly enjoyed the trip home with the rain and Janis and my cold. She slept nearly all day....She was just tickled to see Buster, Midge, and Bimbo, and Horsie. I believe she feels at home, she is so happy.

May 30—[her birthday.] Mother used to say, "Be good on your birthday and you will every day of the year." So I did. We took Clara and Ole home and had a short visit with Mother. I had meant to put out plants but that will wait until tomorrow. I copied three sheets of essays on the typewriter. Myrtle expects a baby. God carry her through for the children need her so badly. I would if we had a capable obstetrician. We have been home two weeks and I have only one lesson in; one more this week-then what? I must get more done....

We went up to Marquette, Monday 27th—That look of surprise and joy as baby drew her breath and held it at Mrs. Higbee's first appearance after five weeks not seeing her. She stayed there the morning while I got a permanent....

Oct. 14—Janis at two years six weeks—Can answer correctly parents name, her own, where she lives, where the Higbees live. She is still in love with them. We were there today where she runs wild with joy....

Nov. 17—Elected secretary of the garden club. Will have to do better than the best to show them my worth. Oh, this lovely music—Frederick Stock of Chicago Symphony—Tchaichowski's Fifth Symphony. Janis can say, "My Shadow" now with some thirty-forty nursery rhymes, and two or three poems ... Higbees are in Florida.

Christmas Day 1935—"There are so many toys, I can barely step."... Last night we took Janis up at 10:30 to enjoy her delight in opening her gifts.... She was completely bewildered until she happened on the the mouth organ, then so far as she was concerned there were no others...We had duck and mince pie. We (Janis and I) took the day off (aside from dishes) and visited Brynhild and ... Daddy at the store....

The one unhappy thought. 5000 killed—many of them faithful innocent servants of our God because of two, (Pope and Musolini) unfaithful servants.

Jan 11, 1936—[They started for Florida and having much car trouble ended up in Escanaba the first night.] Janis all excited about hotel—8 o'clock and ready for bed—Janis read story of "little duck". How I love to hear her untwist those hard phrases. 52 cents for breakfast.

Jan 12—Up at six-breakfast at seven-started at eight-stopped at eleven-65 miles through heavy snowstorm, with very poor visibility-roads slippery-cold wind. I thank God for our stop....

Jan 13—Saw bare spots about today. Pavement bare of snow but wet south of Lake Geneva. Potentially very slippery. Sunday with these many days behind us and so many miles ahead of us. Wednesday we found the roads excellent after the junction south of Chicago Hts. Got into Terre Haute (210 miles) at 4:10. Stayed there all the next day, as we wakened to find the out of doors a snowy fairyland but the roads worst possible. But we were glad to stay and to visit. Zoe [Shriner] gets dearer every year....

After Nashville, it began to snow just as night fell. The hills and roofs were white. When I started up, the car wouldn't go on low, (at gas station) it was so slippery. I could scarcely walk it was so bad. We dared not start today with hills and icy roads. This was once a grand hotel. The windows-panes in dining room 10 feet high, 3-4 feet wide. Balconies on two floors. But rooms shabby. Food good but expensive. Darkies at every hand. Janis lost Ducky Book.. How we dote on hearing Janis read it. Daddy said he wouldn't lose it for a dollar!!

Jan 25, Sat.—In Florida....Moved in, which included unpacking.

Sunday—...Took Janis to the beach. Her face was as solemn as could be, all the while seeing the nearly forgotten things which were so familiar to her a year ago. But after coming home she recited every detail of her trip to us, even to the wiping her feet to get the sand off. This morning she got up, turned on the bathroom light, got completely dressed by herselfwithoutwaiting for us to get up. How sweetly her hair curls.

Florida, 1936.

April 19, 1936—This has been a terrible winter all over the country- floods-snowstorms-wind-record cold-ice-suffering-destruction everywhere—

For us it has been a very pleasant time-in Florida with $3.50 worth of wood to keep us warm and a radio. (Heard Toscanini, Hoffman...)

April 30—Arose at dawn—started at 7:40. [For home]...(Written 6 months later).Shriners in Terre Haute, Ind...intense fog in Elgin, Illinois. Upset me the rest of the way home. We loved Aunt Alice. [Appleton, Wisconsin.] How badly she felt that we found her flat in state of housecleaning....Rode home thru lovely spring night and Janis heard the frogs say "knee-deep," as she and Mr. Higbee [had] talked about. That I were a Psalmist to Praise God for our safe and pleasant trip. That is how I felt as we drove up in front of the store.

May—cold and clear. June fine-still a bit cold. Went to Marquette. Mr Higbee abed with strained back. Janis loved and coddled him—covered him—so full of sympathy and love was she. We exchanged our sentiments—I will never forget his dear self—He has helped me in faith and loving spirit.

I kept busy learning to sew this summer. Worked so hard I had little time to wear dresses. Was self-conscious in the ones I did wear. Spent much time outdoors. Drove to Myrtles—Mothers—with Helen Genry...Marie was here ten days. It's no small task cooking and washing dishes for several guests for more than a few days. Tredway stayed three weeks and I never tired of him, but it was nice to be alone again.

September wet—Mr. Higbee's death—October fine. Many beautiful days. [At this point Alice waxes eloquent about Janis' abilities etc. and then adds:] Sundays she keeps Daddy busy for hours playing with her. She thinks he stays home purposely to play with her. Shuffleboard, building blocks, marbles, ball, reading....

Ella came in December. Daddy likes to see her eat with so much enjoyment. She is happy so long as she is busy and warm. It makes me cross about her not getting out more. One needs to be alone.

I have a big wish for a sewing machine-and vacuum cleaner, Daddy a car-Packard.

Written Nov. 25, 1936—Got the car—Olds. Didn't use it much until this trip....Got vacuum for housecleaning. A pleasure to use it. Janis can clean the dining room alone with it and thoroughly.

May 1937—...Mrs. Higbee stopped with family on birthday....Garden in order early June. Janis ran away. Only severe spanking and punishment made her dependable. No longer afraid of children and dogs. Let her meet Daddy and do errands.

At this point, I believe Alice was pregnant with me. What I understood caused such intense illness with this pregnancy, was gestational diabetes.

June—Felt badly.

July—Very ill all through month. Mrs Higbee helped....

August—Better last part, but weak and helpless. Tredway coming in late made it hard to get proper rest.

September—Doing my own work. Tire easily.

October—Sewed, sewed, sewed ... Mother kicked by horse. Hospital.

November—Mother with us first week—too sick. Dear Mother always afraid she's in someone's way. Worried so for me those last few days.

Florida trip 1937

November 8—Started out at 8:45 am. Arrived at Plymouth an hour after dark—5:45pm. Made good time, 260? miles. Very hard west wind all way from Escanaba. Rain-mud all way to Escanaba. Lunch of oatmeal bread and apples, coffee and candy. Supper at Aunt Alices. Sleep at Curtiss Hotel $2.50. Aunt Alice weak from operation, very tired. We'd feel guilty to stay there or even to stay late to visit.

Nov. 9—Breakfast at 6:30. Aunt Alice at 7:15—She would like Janis if she were orphaned. May God place her in the right hands. I hope she will be taught all the religions and be able to chose later....Hope to be at Shriners tomorrow pm [in] Terre Haute.

Nov. 10—Arrive at 2 pm 196 miles. After good lunch in Turkey Inn. Stayed all day for the fun of it on Nov. 11....

Nov. 14—In Florida...Janis unwell. Tourist home built before war..Janis up to Dr. Black. Tonsilitis...Rented Opgar's 5-room cottage for $350 [6 1/2 months] or $60 per/month. Newly furnished waxed floors, new rugs everywhere, new small gas stove, Frigidaire, fireplace—same as our honeymoon year only seems so much cleaner or more easy to keep clean than then. $43-total cost of trip.

Thanksgiving day in Florida. Cheerless rainy day—65 degrees, but happy and thankful withal. Cozy cottage—all well [with] my doctor here. Good reports of hospital—happy as family....How much of a luxury the sunshine is. Am knitting as much as I can. Have been in looking at baby things. Must knit or buy something for Clara's baby. Dear God, keep her safely in Thy care, and Mother, Charlie, George, Myrtle, James, Jack and all of them.

Jan. 7—Janis had her tonsils and adenoids out. Dr. found it was the right adenoid that had caused the trouble with her ear and breathing. She was very sensible and good about the whole thing. Now she is better and is putting on weight fast. She went into the water and had a glorious time Saturday.... If anything should happen to me. I wish that Owen might get Aunt Alice to live with him and take care of children and leave them to her with enough income to keep them. He would like her—she would love the children. Boy? Ben Owen Tredway—Girl? Palma—

April 18—Easter Monday—Here I sit dreaming when there is so much to write. Tarpon golfing today—Mrs. Higbee stayed with the babies today and spent her time entertaining Janis. She spent a lot of time with her while I was in hospital, too. I went there Feb. 11—Friday. Baby girl born at 12:20—after much noise on my part because of too little confidence in the hospital. I was afraid Doctor Black would not come in time. The greatest thrill of my life time—feeling the baby be born—the greatest disappointment when Dr. said "It is a girl." But no longer is she so. It is nature that we must love them girl or boy. She is a fine healthy baby—perfect in every repect and I thank God a thousandfold for her just as she is. We must take her picture tomorrow up to the hospital where the pretty palms are, after which we named her....I shan't soon forget those eleven days. We were happy there, though I was too sensitive. Dr. Black teased me about not having enough milk. I have [enough] now. I was examined at 7 weeks and announced well, but just then Mother telegraphed that Dad, Papa, she always called him, died on way home from Limestone when he had to go through water. I am glad that he said such nice things to me the morning I saw him last when Mother was with us. Dear Janis said, "now Grandma will be lonesome. We will have to go and see her as soon as we get home." A letter from Clara today, happy baby Sally is.

April 22—Palma smiled at 5 1/2 weeks Cries when she sees me—her milk wagon. Smiles best for Janis. Is sensitive to sound.

Left Clearwater at 8:20 am Sunday morning, May 1st.

May 5—4 o'clock-Otsego. Ellen not home. Went on to Marie's. Children doing work. Marie housekeeper for rich man....Saturday, out to Casnovia. Ella is such a funny dear—and slow. I had to get breakfast if ever we were to leave. Marie brought veal and shortcake out for dinner on Sunday and left dishes for Ella—Mothers Day too....We took prettier route via the lakeshore. Stopped off at Petosky—Tuesday...Lunch at Blaney. Home at 2:30. Daddy went to Ruggles [tooth trouble?], I to see Clara's laughing baby—then cleaned floors. Walked out in crisp air to Helen's.....

Home to see Mother tomorrow.

May 18—Not a word was said at Mother's-[About Grandpa?] Aunt Hannah [Grandma's sister] is very sweet and grandmotherly, generous, and helpful. We brought her back; her and mother. Next day we drove to Rock. Mary Jane and Jimmy fine. Myrtle hustled around and got a fine lunch in a jiffy. Charlie came Sat. to work. Bathroom and Green Room. Yellow room yesterday and orchid room today. Windows washed outside....Charlie worked all day here today....Brynhild here last evening. Daddy trying out hearing devices.

Spring cleaning was a way of life. The coal heating really left a black dust on everything, so every spring all the walls, windows and floors were washed and polished.

May 29—Charles 18—Alice 29—[Both of their birthdays are May 30.] We all were out to Mother's today—24 (of us?) Myrtle's, Clara's, Vivian's, and ourselves. 5 tiny children—Palma, Sally, Mary Jane, Jimmy[Myrtle's daughter and son], and Donald [Vivians son]. We ate the collective Birthday dinner buffet style out on the grass. Cake, rhubarb pie, pork roast, salad, hot biscuits, potatoes, and gravy. Mosquitos worried Janis. We planted Fathers grave the best we could. Drove out to see about Margaret Coaster coming to help me. Has baby chicks, baby lamb, ducks, turkeys. Beautiful driving as leaves are fullout but still of soft fresh green ... Janis ... gets overly excited about little things like I used to. Dr. Black says she's delicately balanced.

Ole, Clara's husband *(l)* and Charlie, mother's brother *(r)*.

Aug. 1—I have been extremely sad this evening. I wanted to visit with someone—Ingid, Alice, Helen. I have been lonesome for Helen.... Instead I played a few old songs which only reminded me of Papa, Louise, school days, home and when Owen and I were in love. Oh, that we could be again. I love him so hard that it makes me ache. I crave his love and he seems so indifferent. He says he loves me as before but I do not believe it when he scarcely notices me for days. I know I'm partly to blame. I let myself become plain. My life has become one round of rounds. It does not seem worthwhile to do anything. We used to sit together so happily evenings. Now he sits by himself. I hope I shall find a way out.

Janis said, "When we see a Negro in the South we do not make strange eyes at him as we do when we see one in the north." She is always reasoning something out to add to our table conversation. Palma sits alone and straight—has begun to eat....I have been happy about my growing friendship with Clara—wonder why it has almost ceased with Helen....Mrs. Higbee is the perfect guest. Knows when and what to help and when to sit down or go out-and when to go. Tredway here again. Gwinn now. Dorothy came over often when he was here. We all like Tred.

Aug. 28—...Janis is correcting her bad habits of crying and scolding with hearts in her diary for each day she controls herself. Palma still airs her lungs when I put her to bed.

Mother always said that I cried all the time. Janis was probably acting out as I take up mother's time. I was told I went on a hunger strike when I was weaned, I'm not sure at what age.

Nov. 13—Palma nine months old. She creeps, still cries for fun....She tastes any food before she will eat it. When she wants attention she fairly screeches until she gets it. She wants to be around where the family is. Janis enjoys her kindergarten and will gain a great deal with so fine a teacher as Miss Leece....

New Year's Day 1939—Janis is just writing in her diary... but finished before me. We had a most beautiful Xmas season and December in general with our first real cold and storm coming the week after Xmas. Mrs Higbee was here then. Janis had Sunday School here with me today as she doesn't seem to want to go to church. Palma tries to do all sorts of tricks that a 10 month baby will and is certainly fun to watch. She eats and drinks like anyone—the only problem at present is to keep her clean and warm on floor where she must be to keep her whole.

Palma in sleigh

My first thought when I saw the sentence about me being on the floor was that I was happy there having my freedom, not being confined. That still fits me today. I don't like to be confined.

Jan. 8—Janis has stayed in bed nearly three days now to get rid of her third cold-voluntarily which shows something in her makeup not many children boast. Palma full of the dickens—creeps or crawls all around, stands alone when not afraid of falling. Now that I have weaned Palma I'm afraid I will have to get up early with her...I will be glad next month when the sun gets up early too...I guess I need a long walk. Everything makes me blue. Daddy is just as he should be but hears badly.

Feb. 5—Palma is under weight but seems strong. Aside from her egg, milk, cereal, banana and orange, I have difficulty in getting her to eat. Her bowels become upset every so often. That seem to keep her weight down. Perhaps this week she'll show some gain. [I guess this is when I went on strike and wouldn't eat, at one year.]

Feb. 27—Palma gained first time since I weaned her-four ounces last week...always busy and happy on floor...Biggest storm of the year last week. Already exceeded last winter's record fall and it is storming again. We had to get coal in spite of Daddy's precaution to get enough last fall to last the winter. They had to carry it in.

May 7—To date we paid Charlie $26.50 and owe him $30.00 which he wants put in the bank. We have accomplished finishing floors downstairs and they're very pretty... Palma sick all day. Janis went out with Clara at 9:30 and they aren't back yet from the farm....I shall always have nice memories of Charlie being here. He wants to go to Alaska.

July 17—You can really live these beautiful days. Friday pm we spent at Rock River. It always gives me a wonderful feeling to be there on a nice day. The Fourth we had a memorable day. Rode out on Ole's [and Clara's] boat to Murray's Bay where we had a picnic. It was too foggy at Trout Bay to

"White Cloud", Ole and Clara's first commercial fishing boat.

appreciate its beauty. Afterwards we had ice-cream and went to the dock to see the fireworks. Shriners are coming this week....

Sept. 12—Janis is back to school. [Janis says;"She kept me out of school for several days because I was stuttering. She had me read to her every day until I stopped stuttering.!?!] I expect her to be the best little reader in the class....I think the reason mothers have difficulty teaching their own children is that they have so many other things to do that they lose patience themselves....

Palma grows nicer everyday. Sings la la la at her play all day....Feeds herself. Likes to go to bed at last. She and Janis play nicely together.

We have had someone here practically every week all summer. Margaret, Tredway, Ann, Marie, Mrs Higbee, Shriners, Eva. Mrs Higbee the ideal guest. Enjoyed having Shriners especially, even if 12 of us did make it exciting for two or three days.

Radio Programs

Mon.	Tues.	Thur.	Sat.	Sun.
Firestone Theatre Drama—12:00	Information Please	WGN Classical 9:30 Town	9:00 NBC Symph.	Ford Theatre Toscanini
	Meeting 8:30-O.		10-12 Man's F.	

Oct. 23—Charlie redid the bathroom floor. It looked nice. He got a ride to St. Ignace with De Vine thru Mrs. P. at Beach. Dear God, I wish for him something better than war. To have his beautiful young manhood wasted instead of used to make our world better would show how uncivilised we are. My special prayer is for him.

Jan. 14, 1940—...Palma one month short of two years... [mother makes a list of my vocabulary.] When she can't have her way she falls into a heap and cries big tears for just a few seconds. Wants to do whatever I am doing—ironing sewing, cutting, writing, cleaning. What she likes best, playing with sister. What she likes least, having her hair washed. It curled just a bit today and Owen is skeptical about its curling just as he was Janis. She is different than Janis....in behavior-livlier physically....,will not be read to but looks at books with Daddy. She is like her in playing a long time with one toy—sings all day, and keeps happy in her own games. Puts aways things very well.

It makes me uncomfortable here when mother compares me with Janis. I guess the reason I put this in is that it shows mother as she is, very human. That's one of the hardest things about parenthood is just accepting children as they are and not constantly evaluating them.

Feb.25—There are advantages even to being sick. When I was useless 7 weeks, two summers ago, I read all Shakespeare's comedies and enjoyed them as I never can when I am so busy. For the past 3 weeks in bed, I have been catching up with my thoughts and Harpers, Time, etc.

Every so often I come upon an article which clarifies my ideas, crystalizes them like the following which I may reread. "Unfolding Americanism" by W. Harper? What is it?

a. Opportunity limited-
b. Individualism-
c. Democracy limited by
d. Complete system of checks and balances-

What we are striving for is similar checks and balances between government and economic—also between capital and labor. This system makes for delays, and ambiguousness. But if we would insist on honest employees from bottom to top who could see problem clearly we should make much more rapid progress.

And this Chinese gem which Anne Lindberg uses to express her "Prayer for Peace" (675 BC).

"I would have gone to my Lord in need,
Have galloped all the way,
But this being a matter concerns statesmen,
And I, being a woman must stay.
I may walk in the garden and gather
Lilies of the mother-o-pearl.
I had a plan would have saved the State,
But mine are the thoughts of a girl.
The Elder Statemen sit on the mats, and wrangle through a day;
A hundred plans they have drafted and dropped,
And mine was the only way."

...Philosophy in Huxley's satiric novel, "After many a summer". "No real progress can be made on human level because of our ego, only on eternal level or animal level."... (reread sometime). Note-Huxley is very religious-walks 20 miles a day....

Feb. 11, 1941—Palma at three. She seems almost a year behind Janis, mentally-that is. Janis at two was where Palma is now in vocabulary, reasoning, dressing herself, buttoning clothes, lacing shoes. Sally, too, is way ahead of Palma in reasoning. But Palma does have qualities which endear her to us....From morning till night she sings and plays with her teddies. She loves Daddy. Each morning she climbs on his bed and kisses him to awaken him. She always says good-bye and meets him when he comes. She is loving and sympathetic to Janis and Sally. She enjoys playing with them. She has a definite stubborn streak and we have to handle her with love lest we bring it on. She sings in tune every song she hears, perfectly way up to high G—has for nearly a year.

March 8—Today Clara took us out to an icy spot on the big lake and Janis, Palma, and I had skates on and tried skating for the first time. At least we didn't fall down though our ankles wobbled. Ole is staying out to Williams Island fishing thru the ice.

March 9, 1941—It has been a year since I have written anything. Mr. Savaried (young Norwegian) is our new minister. He can say what he wants to say effectively but I find him too pessimistic about the town-surely it is bad enough-but there must be some Christian people here as elsewhere... In the past year my favored candidate Mr. Wilkie was defeated. To me he seemed a happy combination of Abe Lincoln and Will Rogers. To me, the outstanding thing of the year is that a few-more than usual-people are waking up to what is happening in the world and are realizing what the real things that count are.

The things I have enjoyed most-in 1940-Reading: "One Man's Meat" homilies in Harpers by E.B.White, farmer-writer... *Time Magazine*—especially about politics. Readers Digest-(cross section of American Country Kitchen, and Home Grown by Della L. Music: Toscanini—Wallenstein, conductors. Marian Anderson-Flagstad singing. Also listening in on Janis' [piano] lessons by Alice Everett. Letters: from Charlie, Mrs. and Dr. Shriner, Miss Fox, and Louise. Friendships: Clara and Brynhild and Mrs Shantze, who has left for Fort Knox, Ky. Work: sewing (improving) and cooking.

On Janis at 8 years....Daddy and Mrs. Higbee think she

(l-r): Janis, Owen, Palma, and Alice in 1939.

is too noisy—but all children are that-otherwise she is as perfect as a child can be—dependable, truthful, honest, responsible, obedient, helpful, works hard and well and quickly—gets excellent marks in school. Would do better if she had to try harder in next grade up. Clinic...found her left eye short-sighted. and fitted her with glasses. She keeps her room clean—keeps herself clean and neat-cooks one dish a week—plays outside with Palma each day—keeps toys neat—makes bed daily—reads and plays piano for enjoyment, finished first year [piano] book in 6 months. Composed a simple piece for Christmas card to her teacher. She reads third and fourth grade-even fifth grade stories aloud to me with ease and expression of adult....Owen has turned over the house account to me-for experience....

Aug. 27, 1941—Nine years wed—[their anniversary.]

1st year-3 mo. studying-3 mo. in Florida-6 mo. waiting for Janis-born near 1st anniversary-Aug. 25th.

2nd year-part in school -loving and caring for baby-

3rd year-part in Florida-

4th year-part in Florida-

5th year-At home-

6th, 7th, 8th and 9th-devoted to Palma's coming and her dear little self—6 mo. in Florida

On Married Life—at times becomes monotonous—with dishes, cleaning, washing, ironing—At times I envy those who have these things done for them but often wonder if they appreciate their extra time gained thereby. At times tiresome—with child problems cropping up no matter how carefully we try to avoid them and no matter how helpful Owen tries to be. At times it used to be strained—because of Marie and Ella but since Owen has taken my part in the past two years we have had no unhappy experiences. A few times bored—Owen and I get out too little. We require little but some of this would be helpful to both of us—Perhaps this is the only way in which I feel his lack of youth. But heretofore, with our trips south—and our country trips in summer I have not suffered in this way.

Today we golfed—as we have tried to every year on our anniversary when the weather permits. Most of the time it is satisfactory to both—We still enjoy the same reading—music—entertainment—admire the same friends—like the same food—appreciate the same things in the children—agree on the important issues that concern us—seldom quarrel about finances—trust each other—and love each other—are equally proud of our combined works of art—Palma and Janis.

March 10,1944—[She ends this journal with 'Plan' for the next twelve months of self improvements inspired by a book called "I Dare You", by William Danforth.]

The In-Between Years

WHAT I REMEMBER after this time was a normal family life. Mother was housewife, girl scout leader, active in the Methodist Episcopal Church. She cooked, cleaned, gardened, picked berries and canned them and was an all around "Domestic Engineer."

Daddy had the store, and walked to work each morning, strolled back for lunch, and home again in the evening. He began work at 9:00 and he closed the store at 6:00, so we ate in the evening between 6 and 7 o'clock. Janis and I and the neighborhood kids would be out playing, often across the street at the school playground, and mother would ring an old-fashioned hand school bell. That was our signal that dinner was ready.

Our dinner was served in the dining room at a big round, oak table and we each had our own place to sit. The table had a tablecloth and each place had a cloth napkin and napkin holder. After we said grace, we ate, and talked of daily news, national news and any other thing that was interesting. At the end of the meal, we sat until everyone was finished. If we wanted to leave the table we had to say, "Excuse me please." It was all very civilized and formal. That's just how it was. We ate off of real Havalind china, and 100% silver silverware that was from the 1920's. After that, if it was summer, we would go out to play again. If it was a cooler time of the year, we would read or play games.

Joan: [describing Alice's homemaking, when Joan spent time with her in the 70's]...I had been deprived of a variety of tastes and vegetables and she took such a pleasure in introducing me to vegetables I had never had and cooking them.. I can remember her sending me to the market for vegetables and she'd say, " now you pick out the vegetables." When I'd come back she'd say, "Now what did you get?" I'd say, "I don't know if it's a cauiflower or a broccoli." I didn't even know the name for it 'cause I'd been so limited to canned peas, beans and corn. The closest thing to a fresh vegetable I ever had was carrots and celery—-and that was it! She had such fun introducing me to these things—-the joys of eating artichokes, and the proper preparation of it. I also remember her teaching me to make bread.—-Kneading it became a Saturday ritual later on when I lived with her for a while.. We'd make rye bread and "Oh the rich aroma." Alice always slowed the pace down. She'd be preparing brocolli, the bread would be baking and I'd be so hungry and I'd just want to gobble it down but nooo—-, you had to wait until the table was properly set and you sat down to eat.

That brings up another memory of Alice. She'd say, "Would you like more milk?" That came as a shock 'cause—I mean she was going to get up and get me a glass of milk [she laughs]. The concept of an adult getting something for me was totally foreign to me having been brought up in a family of seven. I had to serve my parents.

So here was this wonderful woman, so earthy in appreciation of nature, the richness of foods, and her deep spirituality....

Back to the 1940s—Aunt Clara, Uncle Ole and Sally also lived in Munising. Holidays were spent with them, and in the earlier days, others of the Halstead family. Sally being just my age was a blessing for me. I always had someone to play with!!!

I remember one Easter when I was around five years old, we were at Aunt Clara's for the day. Sally and I asked to go down to the fish house to play. When we got there we found the ice shanty and played house for a while. Then, getting bored with that we opted for adventure and decided to "run away."

Aunt Clara lived in "Brown's Addition", about two miles west of our house, which was in the center of Munising. So when Sally and I set off, we headed towards town. There was a stretch of open highway on the way and as we were walking along the highway there, it was becoming dark. By now we were getting fearful of the consequences of our actions, because we knew what we were doing was wrong. Now that we had made the step though, in our minds, there was no turning back. So whenever we saw lights of a car coming down the road, we just jumped off the road into the bushes and ditch that were

Sally pushing Palma on swing.

alongside the highway. That way, we figured, if they were looking for us, they wouldn't find us. They were looking, and they didn't find us. We decided to go to my house 'cause we were getting hungry.

This took us quite a while and we were getting really tired, hungry, and scared, as that's a long way for such little girls. But what a relief when we finally reached the Tredway house and went in. The adults walked in a little later and there we were, sitting on the couch. Talk about upset. Well you can imagine their worry at losing two little girls after dark for about two and a half hours. I think it was about 8:30 when they found us. Our punishment was that we were forbidden to see each other or stay together for a month or more. We were willing to take our punishment because our little rebellion had gotten out of hand. This was not the first or the last trouble Sally and I got into. For some reason, our two energies together always spelled trouble.

I remember going shopping with mother in downtown Munising. We always walked with me skipping along beside her. It was only three blocks and since this was during the war (World War II),

Clara with Sally, Palma, and Janis in sled.

there was gas rationing. During that time there was a big shortage of gasoline, sugar, beef, rubber for tires, and other things. You had to have coupons to get these things. So anyway, we'd head out to Belfry's meat market first. There, mother bought a lot of liver, kidneys and heart as that was what was most available. She had a tight budget and so we ate chicken, pork or beef only for special occasions. From Belfry's we would head for the grocery store, maybe the A& P, and get the stuff needed there. If we had time, we would go to Daddy's store. That was one of my favorite things to do. I could browse the display cabinets, which had all that neat stuff like perfume, clocks, candy, and lots of other good stuff. I could also go behind the counters and to the back of the store. They were busy talking and didn't pay much attention to me so I had the run of the place. I remember it making me feel important.

> *Tredway*: [Telling about Owen, and Tredway's Pharmacy, probably in the mid 30's.] He took me down to the store and showed me how they developed pictures down there. People brought their pictures down to the store and they developed pictures right there. They had a dark room and I was immensely interested in this process and I remember him going to the cash

register and showing me either a five dollar or ten dollar coin, a gold piece. And he said, "You don't see these very much anymore and they're not in circulation much" but they did still use them. He would faithfully send me a Tom Swift book on my birthday or the Bobbsey twins. I liked those books as I loved to read.

Owen's nephew L. Tredway Haglund. 1945

Another thing that we used to do was go on picnics. During nice weather Mother would pack up a picnic and away we would go to some beach, river or Rock River. Mother and Daddy would enjoy the beauty and peace and quiet, while Janis and I would play in the water or on the beach. Pooh Sticks was one of our games we played when there was a bridge. We each dropped sticks upstream of the bridge and the stick that reached the other side of the bridge first was the winner.

Joan: Alice had a wonderful sense of aesthetics for the outdoors. She'd take me out and show me things in the woods, taking me on rain hikes and introduce me to textures and colors, sights and smells...enjoying its essence...bringing out that side of me and feeling really enriched by that experience.

I can just remember the first rain hike she took me on. We had planned to go on a hike on a Saturday—and then it was raining so she said, "let's go on a rain hike." So being a great adventurer, (I'd never been on a rain hike as I'd always stayed in the house when it rained), I went. How much fun it was, how it darkened the colors and made everything sharper, the smells more intense. So after that I can remember many times going on my own rain hikes and not shying away from the rain.

It was just so wonderful to sit on a rock somewhere with her and look out at—-it seemed like the ocean but it was Lake Superior—-or sit and look at a waterfall.. It was all so beautiful.

I interviewed Bernice Williams, a friend of Mother's for many years, and my first music teacher. Her story about how she got to know Alice shows mother's generousity and spontaneity.

Bernice: I've known Alice since May, 1943. I first knew her as a parent in the school, there in Munising, when I was a teacher. You girls were interested in music lessons although we did not begin that right away. What cemented our relationsip was at our first parent/teacher meeting the school nurse talked about communicable diseases and [for] parents to be sure to check their children so they wouldn't spread. After coffee and goodies, somebody said to me, "It looks like you've got the measles." I laughed and somebody else came along and said "What have you got?". It [the measles rash] must have come out just during the meeting,'cause nobody said anything to me at the beginning of the meeting. So the school nurse came over and said, "Yes, you have the measles."

My landlady, who lived about ten blocks away, was there because I had her son as a baritone student in the band. She said to me, "Well, you're not coming back to my house." I don't remember for sure whether it was Alice or Mrs. P. who gathered all my stuff and brought it all over to Alice's house. There I reclined for two weeks or so and I still was not recovered but I was well enough so that my dad came, from Negaunee. He got me and all my junk, 'cause I had been kicked out of my rooming house. I was there for another week or more, I think I was out of school almost four weeks with the measles. I was

> wondering if I'd get called back or not, but I did. I enjoyed it [staying with Alice] very much and of course that cemented my relationship with Alice. Because of her kindness, I got to buy vitamin pills from her husband from his store and teach her two lovely, delightful, gorgeous daughters. [I, of course got measles from Bernice and remember it specifically 'cause it was in the spring and I couldn't go outside.]
>
> I think I had a few other students, who I could not fit in the school schedule so I think I taught at least two or three of those students in her home. I remember Palma sitting on the stairs listening to some of the lessons. Do you remember that? [I don't recall it specifically but I do know I never wandered too far if there was music going on. I am still drawn to music.]

When I was seven or eight, Mother took on a Girl Scout Troop, girls three years older than I was. She became very involved and did trainings and took this all very seriously. I got to go to the meetings and activities and work on the badges with the older girls. I loved it, as mother made it very fun. We did a cooking badge and we served a dinner for the girls' families. The first aid was real exciting for me. I felt really grown up performing artificial respiration. In those days you pushed on the chest rather than mouth to mouth, so we actually practiced on each other.

She taught us square dancing and had a big square dance party where we all wore swishy skirts for our twirling. For the biking badge, we all biked the seventeen miles to Rock River and then stayed overnight in one of the cabins there. These are the activities that stand out in my mind. I'm sure though that we made block prints to make our own wrapping paper for Christmas and possibly spray painting evergreen branches to make Christmas cards. Whether this was for girl scouts or what we just did at our house I'm not sure. But I remember that mother made these things fun.

Everything about our life seemed very middle class and "normal". From my current perspective, though, I know that we had some aberrations. The main one was our inability to express and release emotions. I believe this was the result of Mother's alcoholic family background, where the emotional displays of the alcoholic release the emotions of the rest of the family and so the family never learns skills for processing and releasing emotions. This seems to be a common theme in my Al-Anon groups. (Al-Anon is a group for the families of Alcoholics.) So in our family, we stored up our feelings and they came out in episodes of screaming, crying and carrying on. I don't remember my father participating in these displays but they were prevalent with Mother, Janis and me.

Palma with Janis reading.

I've been asked, "How did your parents get along?" I remember them being very loving and caring for each other. Daddy would give Mother the husbandly peck when he left for work. Mother sometimes stroked Daddy's shoulders and touched him lovingly and they were always very polite to each other.

Aunt Jackie says, "I remember one time when your mom was trying to get your dad to go to a farewell party for the minister at the church. After much pleading by your mom, Daddy said emphatically, 'No, I'm not going!' Later she told me, 'That's the only argument we've ever had.' "

So our life went for these in-between years but things changed overnight.

Mother had an inguinal hernia and had to go to the hospital and have it repaired. Janis stayed home and took care of the house, cooking, etc. as she was 15. I went to stay at Aunt Clara's and thought this was great, although I was a little homesick.

So on the morning of December 18, 1948, Alice was told that Owen had passed away.

Aunt Clara had to tell me that my dad had passed away during his sleep. Evidently, he had complained of gas the night before and when he didn't come down to breakfast, Janis went to wake him up and found him dead. Cause of death was a heart attack. What an experience for Janis, a 15-year-old!

Meanwhile at the hospital, my mother, recovering from her surgery, was in a state of shock. While in the hospital before Owen died, Alice had asked for "what Jesus found." In return she had given to Him "all that I ever was or ever would be."

Coming home from the hospital, I remember her crying a lot for the rest of that year. It was not a fun time for Janis or me either. Our lives had changed overnight and Mother took the rest of that year to make decisions which would make big changes in her life. She was at a crossroads in her life and was now able to continue pursuing "what Jesus found" and her career, which I will chronicle in Part II of this manuscript.

PART TWO

1948 TO 1987

A scan of one of Alice's paintings from the 1970s.

Starting a New Career

IN THE FALL OF 1949, Janis and Mother packed up and headed to Boulder, Colorado in our '38 Olds, to attend school at the University of Colorado. Janis was just sixteen and was to be a freshman. Mother was pursuing a course in counseling.

Alice in Boulder with1938 Olds

Janis lived in the dorms, and mother lived in a rooming house. Meanwhile, I stayed on in Munising in the house at 115 E. Chocolay St.

Mother had put the house in the care of two teachers that she knew, Helmi Harkala and Ursula Utley. Mrs. Utley, as I called her, was an older woman with grown children. She taught Mathematics at the High School and was quite traditional. Miss Harkala was unmarried, also older, and a little more liberal. She taught English. So, not only was the house in the care of these two women but I was also in their care. I was eleven and mother left me in Munising because I didn't want to leave my friends.

The previous year I had spent much time by myself and with my friends. I had always come and gone as I pleased only telling mother where I was going. I had to be home for meals, do the chores required of me but pretty much I was on my own, especially when mother was grieving during that year. So when I was left with these ladies, I expected to be able to have the same freedoms. The problem was that Mrs. Utley wanted to monitor and curtail my actions. So for the first time in my life, I became sneaky.

Since this is a book about Alice and not about me I won't go into a lot of detail here but to consolidate this year into a few words, it didn't work out too well.

At Christmas time, I travelled by train, by myself, all the way to

Boulder, Colorado. I believe Aunt Clara and Uncle Ole drove me to the train station in Escanaba to catch the train to Chicago. I boarded the train late at night and arrived in Chicago early in the morning where my cousin Tredway met me and entertained me until later in the day when I would catch the train to Denver. He entertained me by taking me to his laboratory at Northwestern University, where he was studying to be a dentist, and promptly set me up to fill a cavity in between my front two teeth. I still have that filling although I'm getting it refilled soon, after almost sixty years!!

Anyway, that afternoon I boarded the Pullman car on that train to Denver. My cousin asked two older ladies to keep an eye on me and away I went. I remember crossing the Mississippi River which was very exciting to me. I remember getting into a top bunk, which was made up for sleeping, later in the evening. Also I recall a splitting headache, probably due to not enough sleep, the higher altitude of the Colorado plateau and so much excitement.

Mother and Janis met me in Denver, in our old '38 Oldsmobile, and we headed to Boulder where we all stayed together in a motel room for a week. We went out and got a small Christmas tree and we hung Christmas cards for decorations. I was very happy to be with my family again. We did some sightseeing up in the mountains. I remember going up and up and up to the Continental Divide, all the time mother worrying about the car overheating. We walked a lot in Boulder, up and down many big hills. We ate at the boarding house to see how mother lived. Then back to Denver and onto the train home. I guess that part of the trip was uneventful as I don't remember it.

By the end of that school year there was a real war going between me and Mrs. Utley. I was sneaking and lying and she was restricting and scolding and was I glad when Mother came back home in the spring.

I guess she was returning from Pendle Hill, a Quaker Retreat Center in Pennsylvania where she had gone to study after Christmas.

The following is taken from her book *MAN CAN*.

"I went to Pendle Hill where I experienced Silent prayer and books galore on the subject of prayer loaned to me by the director. Also my hour a week appointment with Dr. Brinton gave me contact with one who had spent a lifetime in prayer and whose actions were based on prayer. A seminar by Gerald Heard at Pendle Hill gave me specific direction of how to begin."

The following poem was written in the '60's about her time at this beautiful place.

SWARTHMORE WOODS

Spring:
Near the gentle stream
Beneath flowering dogwood
is heaped Swarthmore's junk.
Summer:
Someone's carelessly
discarded Hollyhock seed
has grown August tall.
Fall:
It is now Chipmunk's
haven where he hides acorns;
Also, makes his bunk.
Winter:
Snow alteration
masks Man's rags, bags, tin cans in
white mounds, rainbow ice.

That summer, Janis and I spent a lot of time together. She was my keeper, so to speak. Mother was busy trying out her new prayer therapy, working with a family who was having trouble with mental illness, and away much of the time.

In the fall, Janis went back to school in Boulder and Mother went to Los Angeles to Ron Hubbards Dianetics Course. I stayed in Munising with Helmi Harkala. Helmi and I got along fine but I was lonesome for my mommy. So by Thanksgiving Mother was through with her Dianetics course and was going to practice the therapy with a man she met, I believe at U of Colorado the previous year. He may have been the person who encouraged her to take the Dianetics training. His name was Gordon Beckstead and he had a doctorate in psychology. He had a wife and family, and they lived in Phoenix, Arizona. Mother always sought the protection of someone with a PH.D. in psychology as she didn't have that degree in counseling people.

Dianetic Research Foundation of California
2600 SOUTH HOOVER STREET
LOS ANGELES 7, CALIFORNIA

November 25, 1950

Dear Mrs Tredway,

Mr. L. Ron Hubbard, the Foundation and its personnal wish to take this opportunity to express their appreciation for your efforts and cooperation during the Professional Auditor's Course.

The Foundation congratulates you upon your successful completion of the Professional Auditor's Course and on your certification as a Professional Auditor on November 25, 1950. We feel that you will discharge with honor the obligation that certification presents.

L. Ron Jubbard and the staff of the Foundation wish you every success in your new status as a Professional Auditor.

Sincerely,

Gene Benton, Acting Director of Training

Anyway, Janis wasn't happy in school this year and I wasn't happy in Munising so Mother rented a house in Phoenix. Janis came from Colorado and I came from Munising. This time I flew in a big four-engine airplane. I was twelve years old now and I again took the train from Escanaba to Chicago. When I got to Chicago I had to hail a cab all by myself to take me to Midway Airport. I sure was scared in that big city, by myself, getting on the plane all alone. I was pretty excited to fly though, and enjoyed the adventure. The plane took eight hours, as these were not jets yet. I had just gotten over a cold and with a history of ear problems my ears were stuffed up. The airplane trip and pressure from the altitude caused them to stuff up further. So when I arrived in Phoenix, I could barely hear.

We lived in an old rundown rental, right near downtown Phoenix. Always having lived in the north, I was initiated into the world of cockroaches. Big 'water bugs', poking their feelers out of the bathtub overflow, and small ones after any speck of food left out in the kitchen at night. We were loaned an old junker car, a Ford as I recall. Janis says "It took a quart of oil each time I gassed up and a pail of water every twenty miles." So we set up housekeeping. Janis kept the house, and as winter ended and the cotton needed hoeing, she went out and hoed cotton for fifty cents a round (up a row and back again). I was enrolled in school, a grammar school called Emerson School. It went from kindergarten to eighth grade and I was in the seventh grade. It was a mile walk to school and I was mortified the first few weeks of classes because I was not only a new kid in the middle of the year but I was deaf as a post and couldn't hear teachers or kids when they talked to me.

So mother took me to an ear, nose and throat specialist. They did a bunch of tests, irrigated my sinuses and did more hearing tests and then told mother that I needed to have my adenoids removed if I wanted to restore my hearing.

As I recall, the irrigations did help a little but what happened is that mother put me "on the couch" so to speak, and audited me. Now this was a first for me and it's rather foggy in details after nearly sixty years.

She took me back to something pleasurable. This was stock Dianetics counseling. She'd count backwards, "ten, nine, eight, etc". and say, "What do you see?" I would relate what I saw and then she would direct me again. I may have gone back to a pleasant experience with my father, I don't remember, but I do remember that after a while we were back to my father's death. She had me go through the experience in different ways, maybe at first just reciting what I saw, and then moving through it feeling the emotions. I think I remember crying and mother talking about me "running" off my grief, crying being a way of doing that.. Anyway, within days of this experience, I could hear again. For her own satisfaction, she took me back to the specialist and he was amazed, saying, "Those adenoids are entirely shrunk back to normal". That was my first experience with mother's therapy, but I was to be "audited" many more times in my lifetime.

I think Janis went to this Dianetics course with Mother. If not, Mother shared her experience with Janis and "practiced" this with her. During these early years they took copious notes while they were working on someone.

My next experience was maybe a month or so later. I came home from school with a splitting headache. Janis was the only one home and so she said, "Lay down here on the couch and I'll see if I can help you." She used similar techniques to Mother's and instructed me to go back to an earlier time when my head hurt. Then back to a yet earlier time of this "headache" chain. Each time she would ask, "Where are you?" According to Dianetics, there were psychosomatic chains which were tied to an emotional experience which was associated with a physical pain. These were all tied up together and so every time you had an emotional experience like the first one, you'd get the physical reaction, such as a headache. Sometimes these went back into prenatal periods of your life. All the time Janis was writing this down.

She kept sending me back further and I guess that I started describing this big white house. She asked me where it was, and I didn't know. Janis said, "Going back even earlier, you said you heard someone say, 'Hitch up the horses, Ben.' then you described the store (Tredways Pharmacy) with a feeling of having built it." When mother got home that night, Janis told her about my "session" and about the house. From the description I gave, she was sure it was a house that I had not seen in this life. That of my grandfather in Casnovia. He also helped to build my father's drugstore. So, they decided I had gone into a past life. To my knowledge, this was the beginning of Mother's experience with past lives. According to Mother, I was my grandfather, Benjamin Tredway, in a previous life. I have to say, that I believe that I was, also.

One reason I related with having been my grandfather in a past life was the four poster bed. We had an old four post bed frame which was always admired by every one who saw it. I never could see what people thought was so great about it. It seemed crude to me. One time I asked my mother "who made that bed anyway?" She said, "Grandpa Tredway built it." I said , "Oh, that's why I don't like it. I never was happy with the way it turned out."

Alice on beach at Rock River

I loved living in Phoenix and my new school by now, but as the end of May and the end of the school year arrived, the weather got blistering hot. It was time to go back to Munising. I also assume mother's work with Dr. Beckstead was at an end or we would have stayed longer.

That summer I remember learning how to wash clothes in our old-fashioned wringer washer. I also recall Mother and Janis doing a lot of auditing. I think I was pretty busy with my friends getting into stuff that was probably not that good for me such as smoking cigarettes and maybe even drinking beer.

In the fall Alice started on a new quest to study with a Dianetics Group called The Clearing House, in Florida.

The application for this endeavor is printed below.

The Clearing House: Application

1. Married Aug. 27, 1932. Janis born August 25, 1933. Palma born in Florida Feb. 11, 1938. Husband died Dec. 18, 1948.

2. My attitude toward my father has changed greatly since Dianetics. I hated him for his drinking and swearing (deceased 1938) and unfairness of punishment; I admired him for his Irish gayety, his friendliness, his respect for Mother, his brilliance of mind. Now I understand his shortcomings.

My mother, I always worshipped, and appreciate her now more than ever; for, she practiced Dianetic theory all the time. My husband was as perfect as husbands could be, pre-Dianetics. My understanding of my children has changed greatly since I have audited them and seen what I should have been as a mother. I am not in touch with my in-laws much of the time. A younger sister's family lives here in town, and she is respected by all the family; the daughter has been accepted almost as our own. I respect my sister as the best friend I have. It is very difficult to answer your questions; for I get both answers, pre-and post-dianetics.

3. 4. 5. I was introduced to Dianetics June 1950 by my friend Gordon Beckstead, then a student of the University of Colorado. He sent me to a perfect return to where my father had me upside down saying, "It's a girl…," in the same tone of voice one would say, "It's a million dollars." Well, I was so excited about it I spent the summer practicing on my poor daughter, also my friends. The last of August I flew to Phoenix to study with Dr. Beckstead. We co-audited a bit but felt the training course essential; so we took five weeks of Los Angeles; then we worked together the rest of the year. I returned home in June and found stimulating practice with couples outside of Munising. I have recently introduced the subject to this small town of 4000.

Alice sightseeing in Utah. 1952

I co-audited with Mason Smith this summer who is very successful, and a very good auditor on the amateur basis. I think I have read everything printed by Hubbard and the Foundation including tape recordings of the Convention which Dr. Beckstead still sends to me. Also I have read and appreciated Dr. Winter's book and the papers sent out by the Toronto group, and the Altman group. I have audited approximately 2000 hours, the first eightly of these before certification. I have been an Examiner since the paper was first published; but have continued with processing whenever it was available for me; about once a week. I have been audited 200 hours by Dr. Beckstead (both as student and student-professional) and by Smith (above mentioned) and my daughter, unprofessional. I use Standard, Effort, Emotional Curve, Postulate, my own variations of all of these, and any that seem especially suitable to any particular pre-clear. If the pc [pre-clear] is interested in Examiner I set up that Circuit immediately and then work with E instead of File-Clerk and Somatic Strip. I find it much more efficacious in that with E one can use any type of processing including standard or postulate, and even completely new ones. Also it seems to take care of the need for creative work and play and exercise, and the appetite for specific foods, vitamins, minerals according to what is being reduced.

Dr. Beckstead taught a group last year in Dianetics co-auditing in which I took but a very minor part; also I attended the Phoenix group several meetings and demonstrated once.

In auditing I am very happy and courageous; but in approaching a new pc [pre-clear] I feel very the opposite. My communication is not what I'd like it to be on the interviewing or straight memory level, or in speaking for Dianetics.

6. B.S. and A.B. Northern [Michigan] College of Education, 1934

20 hours toward M.P.S. at University of Colorado, 1950

3 months study of group psychology at Pendle Hill (Wallingford, PA.) 1950

5 weeks at Foundation, Certified November 25, 1950

Three training courses in Girl Scouting

7. Work history includes only one year of teaching; then seventeen years of motherhood and housework; this broken by girl scouting both with adults and girls, in camp and out. My attitudes? Always positive

toward work of all kinds, and children, with a particular leaning toward children of any age. I always enjoyed the variety and informality of housework. My teaching was simply taken as a step toward growing up with the interest in the people involved.

8. Interest NUMBER ONE: DIANETICS. Interest number two: Seeing Palma through. I have some big plans ahead for the young people good and bad but feel that I can make so much faster progress by first preparing myself for the best that is in me. I am Protestant and am interested in some ways in the possibilities of what a United Protestant (not exclusive) or United Church movement could do for a community's young folks of all ages: 3 to 80. I am not anti here; never was. I would take down all doors or leave them all open so that The Church that offered the Most Truth and Most Love would attract the Most People. My accomplishments so far are not worth boasting except for the two fine daughters. I proved to myself and to twenty four girls over a period of four years that Scouting is fun. I have proved to many and to myself that there is Something in Dianetics.

9. Present recreations and amusements; mainly Dianetics. I like to walk, to loaf, to swim, to climb mountains, to garden, to pick wild berries and and can them, to read, to write, to listen to music, to visit with friends, and to pray, Quaker style. I enjoy cooking, sewing, knitting. I like to learn something new.

10. When I was housekeeping I "belonged," but since I have been in training I do not. I go to church and adult classes. Next fall I hope to pick up a few outside interest groups; this year I avoided becoming involved because I planned to be away.

11. Chronic somatics: Past: Menstrual troubles, acne, colds when I got wet feet or lost my sleep, jaundice when I ate fats, a slight astigmatism of eyes, and a "nervous disposition."

Present: no menstrual troubles, only a slight trace of acne, no colds, no jaundice, still the slight blurring when discharging emotion, (eyes), still a slight tension under certain circumstances.

12thru 20. None

21. My flash answer is yes to hypnotism: soft voice when very fatigued in car during travelling. Has not been run off.

22. see 11. also anxieties or fears and doubts have all been run off, mostly by SP; so probably I need remodelling of postulates.

23. Well, of course, running off grief or loss while being processed. Here, by the way, is one way I have probably been helped. I used to cry when misunderstood. Haven't checked these postulates. Will sometime. Also, of course, discharging my husband's death has been a mighty release for me.

24. Attorney George S. Baldwin, Munising, Michigan

Dr. Gordon L. Beckstead, Psychological Research Foundation, Phoenix, AZ.

Dr. George Wickstrom, Munising, Michigan, (friend)

Mrs. Lyndon Miner, 717 W. Vernon Avenue, Phoenix (pre-clear)

25. My interest in Dianetics is manyfold. All my life I've wanted to help out the kids who get into trouble. Many have, through the years come to me. Always I felt inadequate. That is why I took up counseling at the university, and social psychology at Philadelphia. When I came upon Dianetics, I said "this is it." Nothing would do but be processed, learn, practice, and now I'd like to learn again. When I found my purpose in life it turned out to be to help these youngsters. I could see everything I ever really enjoyed doing, helped me...toward this goal. But finding it spurred me to greater effort toward the preparation where I could really do something.

Another great pleasure of mine is an inside understanding of people. Dianetics gets closer to this than anything I found in psychology. It's as good as knowing a child that tells you everything. It is super.

Even though I never practice on psychosomatics after I begin my real work, still, knowing just the right thing to say or ask of people who have these chronic ailments, these neurosis, will help them understand themselves. It helps me love and want to serve my fellow man because I know it is such an easy thing to do via Dianetics.

It makes me so much more effective in my work than I could otherwise be. It surpasses any training given at present in Universities or Prison schools. It makes me well physically, spiritually, and mentally; a whole adjusted person, able to love and be loved, to move and have my being in aberrated groups without myself being unduly disturbed or restimulated.

On the church level it broadens and lifts the mind to greater heights than ever before attained by ordinary people like me. It shows sin for what it is, and cleans up sex for its real purposes; growth, union with life, and creativity whether of life, or of arts. It makes a woman out a of a woman, a man out of a man, and a child as he was meant to be.

I'd like someday to be in a position where I could see what it could do for education.. That is one program that really needs revamping, and I'd like to have a hand in it, with the tool Dianetics, the knowledge Dianetics

First thought of this application; it would assist processing. Next thought; it would be fun to write the answers. Next, it's not organized the way I think, I guess for I've had a deuced time trying to stay with you. It is the best interview I've seen to date, however. Maybe I'm just different. Ha! there's a cue.

It appears that she was accepted as the next correspondence I have is this letter.

February 7,1952

Agnes Fitzpatrick,

Thank you for the beautifully handwritten letter. It gave me a warm glow, and a feeling of friendliness, and of welcome.

The question I would ask is, "How much the cost?" but I have determined I'd get my money's worth out of it where you charge me the learner's fee of $400, or the co-auditor's fee of $200, or compromise on the middle one of $300.

We think we would like to live apart from the Clearing house for Palma's sake who had to take Dianetics in the form of a much restimulated mother and sister during early months of auditing; also she had to be more or less in contact with some pre-clears who came to the house for auditing this summer (from out of town). So, the farther away from the subject she need be, the better. Although at present, she is being audited an hour a week. She dissolved her adenoids and corrected her deafness and headaches thru processing, and is now working on acne. It is not that we want something swanky; it is just that I think it best to take my fourteen year old along with the least discomfort possible for her. Any small modest place that is pleasant and somewhat free from insects is acceptable.

We would like to leave about ten days before the third of March to leave us plenty of time to stop at Tampa, Clearwater, and Winter Park on our way through. Janis remembers Florida and wishes to revisit old haunts and friends. The reason for mentioning it is that you answer the application soon enough for us to register and get ready to go.

As I re-read the papers I just finished writing, I think of something I like about Dianetics. I am able to write anything and know that it will not bother you who read it, only help you to understand my problem, my aberrations that need correcting. Janis just read the application blank and said she liked the questions, and the way you stated them.

Here's to an early meeting with you at The Clearing House.

Dianetically,
Alice Tredway

As you can see we were now ready to leave for Florida. As it turns out, we were there for six weeks. Talk about a fun time for me.

We travelled by car, still the '38 Olds, and, as mother said, saw all the old haunts, such as where I was born in Clearwater and other places Janis remembered. We came down the west coast of Florida and crossed over to the east coast via Alligator Alley. We ended up staying at a place called Briney Breezes.*

This was a small trailer park right across the road (A1A) from the ocean. We were renting a trailer that was perhaps twenty five feet long. Mother slept in the bed in back and Janis and I slept on the foldout couch in the living area. The first day we were there we went to the beach for an hour or so around noon and we got burnt so badly that we couldn't go to the beach for two or three days. This was in the days before sunscreen.

*Briney Breezes the camping resort became incorporated as a village in the late 50's as developers started buying up property on the ocean. Jan and I visited it in 2001 and it was still much like we remembered. In 2007, 84% if the owners voted to sell to a developer, as they were being offered about one million dollars/trailer site. There was a particular feeling of community there that is gone forever.

It was a good experience for me and Janis. We were a part of a community of 'snow birds' of which many had children. Whereas these kids had to go to school, Janis and I got to be 'just beach bums'. In the evenings and weekends we hung with the others. There were bonfires some nights and square dancing in the recreation room two or three nights per week. It was a great experience for me.

I think it was a pivotal experience in mother's counseling career as I don't think I ever heard of her studying Dianetics again. I heard things like, "they are just after money", and other derogatory things said about that group. From now on mother followed her own path which diverged from her beginnings in the Dianetics Fellowship, later called Scientology.

The next school year, 1952-53, Janis went to school in Marquette at Northern Michigan College. I was in the height of my rebellious teens and hated that mother was so weird. She was always "in prayer" and went back and forth from her room to the car. Perhaps this was for a change of scenery, or to give us space in the house. She was telling the minister at the church that he was Judas and had to forgive himself and one night sat in the church praying and refused to go home until they called Janis to come and get her. It was all very harrowing for me, a teenager, to have such a crazy mom. Probably pretty mortifying for Janis too. I guess these were the years that Mother was "finding herself" and developing her prayer therapy.

> *Brynhild*: Once your mother had someone visiting and she took her to the island [Grand Island] on a picnic or something and they danced on the sand. This got around Munising and it was reported that they were crazy. Evidently this person had been having marital problems....Years later mother visited them out west and they were doing wonderfully.
>
> To the Methodists Alice was very interfering. She got into Herbert Ingraham's past lives and Earlene, his wife, got very upset about it. So Alice would go up to the church at any hour of the night and be in the church at night , probably praying for

Herbert and others….So they locked the church doors so she couldn't go there anymore.

E-sessions—Alice started them in the early 50's—Edna, Janice Taff, myself and Alice. Alice or one of us would have someone in mind for us to pray about (we wouldn't give a name)—so we'd all sit silently and someone would say " I see ———— ——" and describe a picture in their head. [For instance, "I'm looking at a glass of water and the light is shining on it and that makes it all sparkly".] Then we'd go around in the circle [continuing that process]….

Sometimes I would just say,"I'm glowing" which is what I did most!! Just supporting is how Alice described it. Then Alice would say, "We'll move to the next person now" and we'd go around the circle a few times for the next person we were praying for. We'd give feelings, pictures we saw in our heads, and thoughts that came to us. We felt that this was valuable to those we put in and also to ourselves.

These E-sessions were the beginning of her symbol sessions which she used throughout her life. The basis of this prayer-therapy is that when a group of people are gathered, they have a group energy of spiritual power. If the group gives up their will to that of the higher power, then the power of the group will be that of a higher power. The symbols that are given then go out to the good of "All" or the the good of members of the group or their families. These are very uplifting, fun and healing sessions. I have been able, on a fairly regular basis, to have these sessions with some of Alice's colleagues since the time of her death. Edna also hosted these sessions at Rock River and requested that they be continued there. That's where I have tried to carry on this tradition.*

---

*From *E-Therapy* by A L Ketselman-"We think that there is an intelligent power within you which can transform you by removing identifications, and we will call this power, "E" or whatever name you prefer.

Paying Her Dues

BACK TO THE '50's—I have journals and some letters from this period. At this time Mother was taking piano lessons at the college in Marquette from Hal Wright and, from Herbert Ingraham in Munising. She was also teaching many young beginning piano students and was quite successful from what I heard from people.

Janis was living at Sand Point in a 35 foot house trailer where her husband Alvin Reffruschinni was stationed at the Coast Guard Station. I was at MSU going to college. I had recently broken up with my high school boyfriend, Carson, but we were still friends and hanging out occasionally.

In the following journal entries I have tried to give you a taste of her continuing prayer and early work she was doing along with some personal aspects of her life.

I can see mother, in the morning, sitting at her teacart which she used as her desk. The teacart was at the east end of the living room and got the morning sun. Every chance she got, she would sit in the sun. This is where she did most of her writing.

In her journals she refers to Janice, Jan and Janis. I will always use Janice for Janice Taff. Otherwise when Mother is referring to Janis or Jan, it is her daughter.

Jan. 1, 1958—Visited with Palma—Rode out to Janis'—Had session for DD [Owen, Janis' son]—Went back through horror of past death in concentration camp gas chamber—Carson, Palma picked me up.

New Years resolution—That I may be worthy of what God asks of me, Jane? Wright? Lyn? George? ESP? Louise?... Edna? Martha? Mary? Janis? Janice? [Praying for these people or working with them, I assume.]

Jan 2—Outline for ESP January and February

1. Clairvoyance
    a. Raking away muck
    b. Experimental
    c. Testing

2. Foretelling
    a. Getting muck out of way
    b. Sharpening senses
3. Telepathy
    a. Peter and Mother
    b. Alice and Janis
    c. Alice-Peter
    d. Alice-Peter-Martha [mothers hairdresser and son Peter.]
    e. Written
    f. Telephoto

Jan. 4—Up at 6:30 am—Walk up Superior St.— [go] to Marquette-[piano] lessons with Dr. Wright....[Dr. Wright taught at NMC in Marquette.]

Jan. 5—Rae Lynn [Janis' daughter] here all day. Jan, Alv, and Owen went to the Light [Au Sable Lighthouse where they had previously lived] after church....Jan and family at Clara's tonight for supper. Later our session on Owen, [and] new baby [Janis is pregnant] and Alice?

Jan. 7—Completely tired after the children today—then Christies lesson and Mary's. [She taught piano to next door neighbor Janice Taff's children, plus many others.] Brynhild came up and we dismantled tree and Brynhild fed branches to fire as I cut them. There is such a sad feeling about taking down the tree that I never can overcome, that I particularly liked B's chattering and warmth.

Jan. 8—The lonesome, sad, feeling of the day of reckoning, going thru Christmas cards and cleaning up decorations—Ironed blouses, practised a little, prayed for three. Symbolism-holding needle over flame of candle. Palma's schedule this term....

Prelude in C minor Chopin—....Five more lessons to learn to play before a critical audience—to learn to hear before a critical audience—to light candle with candle, with fire. [I assume she's preparing for a recital at this time.]

RaeLynn and Owen(DD)

Jan. 11—Asked only to love Christ and let "everything" flow through me today.

Jan. 13—...Janis and Alvin, R. L. [Rae Lynn] and Dat Dat [Owen] here for supper and they to show[movie] after. Then Janice Taff and Janis and I worked by fireplace till twelve.

First—open up more charge on DD's past death (inhumanity, trapped, poison.) Then Alice sub-conscious-3rd century "shaman" "fakir" —cobra, tiger, et al.

When Mother "worked," she had her helpers give symbols, and she went into the past lives of, in this case DD and herself. Also she would go into valences. By this she meant that she went into another entities persona and saw things from that perspective.

Jan. 14—Kids slept thru till 6:15. We got up at 6:30...Rae Lynn and DD pasted into scrap book. Lunch-then Mrs. Reff's lesson. Gabbed an hour, then slept off poison of DD's.... Supper of wine, warmed potatoes, onion and fresh mushrooms....Then piano-[practised]. Really nice letter from Palma.

Jan. 17—Prayer and Prayer—Practise and Practise....Bed at 7:30—Prayer all night.

Jan. 30—Palma writes of her many dates—and the variety of men she is meeting—now one—Big Swede and German she calls Dutch seems to fascinate her and please her with his interest in music.

Feb. 3—Just sat—hour upon hour by the window and

received the love of Trinity—preparing for evening session on Elijah, [Mother always said she was Elijah. Janis explains it, "In a spiritual sense, her mission was as Elijah's was the "role of Prophesy".] and Wright [her music teacher.]...Evening session...understanding about Wright's responsibility to clear up my peace with God—on Elijah.

Feb. 18—Jan stayed over—in state of impatient waiting. [For her third child to be born]—Children fun in snow banks and riding on shovel. Prayer given for Jan till noon then for H. W. until 8—then for Alice until noon Wed. Palma called—talked long time—in love with Dutch?—wants my approval but I felt teasy and lectury???

Feb. 24—Started morning in prayer—Jan and Alvin left babies off so that took care of rest of day....Jan stopped to "tell" Rae Lynn and kiss them good-bye on way to hospital. David born at 11:40 pm. 8lb 11 oz. Brynhild stayed with children while Alv and I stood by.

Feb. 27—Sent special delivery letter to Palm giving her full freedom including freedom to marry any time—also note and blue slip to Mrs. Petit [housemother at dorm] for Palm's permission to leave town after dance.

Feb.28—Continued absorbing darkness—headache and heaviness. Broke fast at suppertime....Janis and three babies went home to "little trailer house."

March 1—...Palm and Dutch [Kermit Richardson] called in evening and said they had been married day before-Feb. 28, at 5:30 by Methodist minister. Dinner with Barb [my roommate] and friend. Went to Spinsters Spin [MSU formal dance], stayed in motel overnight and then spent week-end in Monroe. [with Kermit's family.]

March 12—Forgiving humanity for "ingratitude." Giving up my own stupidity, human-ness folly, all postulates from the beginning, that interfere with my new conscious choice of "union with God."...Erasing "Abjectness" the folly in humans. Erasing all postulates, thoughts or feelings on all levels of consciousness that might interfere or cause resistance to God (All)'s flow and Will through me—since beginning includes postulates made by human race since I also accepted these. [Trying to get out of her own way in her quest for "union with God."]

March 21—Worked hard,...washing up, cleaning upstairs, front hall, bathroom, ironing curtains, in preparation for Palmas and Kermits coming. [Kermit meeting family for first time.] They came about seven—had supper—drove out to Jan's on muddy road. Had fun—all relaxed and laughed and got acquinted.

March 22—Love Kermit more every minute. Jane reports week by week iumprovement—absence of fear—toning of muscles in good leg—more confidence in using it and getting around. We got to bottom of her fears today—which are to be completely released by next time. [Jane had polio as an adult and was partially paralyzed. Mother seems to be working with her regularly.]

March 31—Blue day—Think it was because I knew Jan would not be in—Shovelled two feet of snow off length and breadth of sidewalk. Took two hours. Day was so perfect I just had to be in it...

April 1—Still running "Semmelweis", story of doctor who intoduced asepsis into medicine, eliminating death from childbed fever in his own and associates practice, but who broke down because of supposed failure to have his findings put into practice. I am to learn "holy indifference to success or failure in all my work in order to use the 'wasted energy' of the emotion resulting from failure or success." As Tao says—when one of Tao finishes a task he withdraws, skipping both laurels and abuse.

April 2—...Still running "Semmelweis" until four today. Then "holy indifference." Gave in to my weakness of wanting marshmallow chocolate sundae—but was duly and properly disappointed. My taste has changed since "Leslie" days. Met tonight with Edna, Beo [Brynhild], and Janice [e-therapy group]. Entered W's help. 14 entered. [A prayer group operating by giving symbols for the persons entered into session.]

When Mother talks about 'running' or 'running off', I understand her to mean that she is letting that energy flow through her to the'All' for healing. In this case it seems she is running her own emotions of success or failure in her life and work.

April 20—Piano, and loafing. Back to egg diet—I feel like an elephant at 156. Just thirty pounds too much in the middle. Why not just go without food for thirty days? [Mother struggled with her weight all through these next years.]

Three children here to nap while Alv and Janis went to show [movie] "Ten Commandments." I might go again.... Went with M and L a year ago. God says, "that was age of Miracles: this is age of Love.

May 1—Asked God what I had to lose if I got thin?—answer—"Mortality." First we seek Immortality to the tune of thousands of churches, shrines, ministers, priest in monasteries, temples etc. Then when offered we resist! On way out to Jan's Rae Lynn said, "I come back with you affer, Alweis?" So she was here till noon today. We ate regularly this week-so-on the scales at noon 160. I know it is from being in restimulation this week since I have been erasing resistance in eight lives—to thinness—survival charge—four of them in lives with G B.

This reference to erasing resistance in eight lives is exemplified in the following poem. Her poem is one of her past life stories and how she sees, with humor, one aspect of her soul and karma. She saw herself as Edgar of this poem.

THE GHOST OF SALEM SQUARE

Our hero is Edgar from London fair
Who was dashing and dancing and debonair;
Whose comely face and carrot redhair
Lit up the church in Salem Square.

I Remember Alice

He'd apprenticed to organ and carillon,
Bound over to a Belgian named LaBrun,
Who loved him, pampered him, called him "My Son."
"Old Master, I say, you're the best in Town."

He learned right quickly his lessons on organ
And bell. He maneuvered with skill
The fine glockenspiel. He liked to run
Errands from high authority won

Praise and the promise of Church and State;
Prominent officials said he would rate
A position as musician, partner and mate
Of the Carillonneur at an early date.
His thoughtful ways and natural grace,
Kind manners, softened the cruel stern face
(Encircled in the finest of imported lace)
Of the priest, Dean Penrick who ran the Place.

Our story is laid in 1692
When charmed lives there were but few
Who missed the Hangman, the empty pew,
Or Dungeon. Young men were said to brew

Heresy. So with our hero who walked
One morning through the square and talked
To a witch who was chained there. He balked
At all Laws, angrily swore as he stalked

To the Office of the Church and loudly demanded
Of Reverend Penrick that her case be remanded,

She be given a fresh trial. He shouted, commanded.
Promptly in the cold deep cellar he landed

To await his own trial. Through heavy walls
Of stone he heard the familiar bells,
Ring for her burning. His wailings and calls
Ignored except by the rats in the stalls.

"Surely, my neck's cinched in the noose,
Hanging limp as a Christmas Goose.
I should have known better than to let loose
My temper at Devil Penrick's abuse

Of Authority; for, he would certainly smother
And torture in flames, his own father or mother,
As earlier he did my favorite brother.
I must be the fourteenth, Just another

Ordered deader than dead by him,
I'm sure, according to his sacred whim,
He'll find he cannot punish or fetter
A soul. I'll torment and tax his forgetter
By sending him a daring letter,

Setting forth my purpose and plans as a ghost."
In due time our hero was a gallant host
To Two Thousand who sooner or later would boast
Their great self-righteousness. Almost

It would seem as he hung from the oaken beam,
A smile shone and in his eyes a flame

Of malicious mischievousness.. "I'm here to redeem
The fourteen lives you've taken. My steam

You'll shortly feel under you. Your shrine
Will be hell as I tinker, twist and twine
The ropes of the glockenspiel. No wine
Will tempt. You'll be too ill to dine.

The organ will heave, bellow and blare
During your most solemn and reverent prayer,
Your candle'll either grow dim or flare
Wildly. Whether wheat or tare

You'll care long before I'm through."
The gardener-hangman, as if he knew
Buried him deeply. "There, you'll do,"
Planted flowers to improve the view.

So Edgar, our hero, (this writer was he,)
Shortly returned as a ghost, circumspectly
Tampered the bells, set prisoners free,
Worried the Dean, upset his tea.

Though dancing, and dashing and debonaire,
He startled the Dean with his fiery stare,
In work, in thought, or even prayer
The Dean was not free from Ghost Edgar.

May 3—Marquette for lesson in '37 Olds. Got there and back too. Lunch at Rock River. Worked with Jane on feeling in right leg.

May 9—Working to erase imbalance of emotion as I relate myself to God. Jan and babes were here all morning-Brynhilds and TV at night.

May 18—Out to Rock River for session with Edna "climbing Jacob's ladder"-

1st rung	"personified faith"
2nd	"
3rd	accepted love
4th	quested beauty
5th	direct contact.
6th	healing

[This Jacob's ladder later becomes some of her "steps Godward."]

June 6—Myrtle [her sister] Pat and Ruth [nephew & wife] here till two. We worked in sunny backyard with Myrtle till noon then listened to Pat make recordings of his guitar and singing.

June 30—Busy each day this week housecleaning in expectancy of Palma coming home. Accomplished: Clean green room; wash and wax floor in Jan's room; wash front porch and scrub hall and kitchen. Thorough vacuuming with new Electrolux.

July 4—Parade—Clara came up after [The Fourth of July is big in Munising]. Kermit and Palm here till 3. Bernice and Jack & children came for first visit in two years. Jan and Alvin came in after for supper. I had first chicken in six years—no special pleasure.

July 20—One half hour of prayer after breakfast every day. Began June 17.

"Dear Father, I present my soul for this day – for thy Glory- my brain for complete restoration, my body for transfiguration. I present my action, thoughts, words, for thy glory. I present thy purpose and plan for Munising, for the Kingdom, for thy twelve men and their families. I present C-P-J-J-D-S-P etc. for special Blessing, thy perfect grace. I wait upon thee—More simply I present my soul, this day to thee and all thou wouldst do with it for thine Glory."

[As Alice is "working on herself, she is developing her format for her "life readings" which are her outline when taking people into past lives later in her work. The following appears to be an early outline of her own "life reading."]

Oct. 18—Alice- Choices-
1.—to be-
2.—series- insect –furry animal-child-
3.—man is redeemed by love-
4.—God (at death 12th century)
5.—Freedom-truth 6th and 7th century when imprisoned Truth 1942
God 1948
Purpose of love———love
In the beginning is God –Is Love? Answer—not all
Will there be love? All
Man or God made? Both
Man adds to love even as Christ
Everyman add same? No

1. understanding
2. beingness
3. strength
4. creativity
5. warmth
6. beauty
7. harmony to love
8. purity to love

Definition of God——*God is*—(All the rest is manisfestation)…
Agreements—1946—To know God as Christ knew Him.
Breaks-(4)
1-self- 12th century broke with truth
2-broke with man 1692—[Depicted in poem "Ghost of Salem Square"]
3-broke with life—Huron Indian-don't want to look at it
4-can't see beauty of it…

Oct. 26—Took kiddies to H G's while Alvin and Janis went to 10 o'clock mass—Alvin to communion. Afternoon visited Brynhild, worked in yard, doped awhile. [Sleeping as a method of "running off" aberration.] Walked with Brynhild. Beautiful moonlight and warm evening.

Principle breaks-Anyone—-

With self	Mankind
life	Spirit
time	Christ
Beauty	God Father
Love	God All
Truth	Purpose
Universe	Reality

Alice Affairs—

1-Give God	Household affairs
2	Money
3	Marriage
4	Social
5	Life Purpose
6	Music
7	Creativity
8	Speaking Assignments
9	Writing
10	Transportation Problems
11	Family Affair

Each night running off basic breaks.

Nov. 4—Letter from Palm at last. Kermit got my private letter to Palma and read it first-in which I suggested Palma's headache to be restimulation of her choice to be a woman in this life and now doesn't like being pushed around by a man. [This is the beginning of mothers and Kermits animosity to each other.]

Nov. 23—Heard Bert's [Methodist minister] sermon on forgiveness and healing. True as far as he knows but, he knows so little without recognizing our monstrous and beautiful past of evolution of soul as well as mind and life form.

Nov. 26—Not much of anything but washing clothes and me of my sins of judgment of self and others....erasing charge on hands [her hands were stiff with arthritis at this time.]—judgement-unforgiveness connected with H. W. and self—on hanging and playing organ –1692.

Dec.2—...Walk with Brynhild—every scene looked like Christmas card—was ecstatic over dozens of scenes on this soft snowy night—

March 9, 1959—Students as usual. Freddie really reading now. [Music, I assume.]

March 18, 1959—...Helen V. has been home here with her parents.(Mrs V. broke her hip in Nov.) We spend nearly every evening from 9-12 together sitting by fire or playing scrabble or viewing Sunday TV at Brynhilds house. Jan and I still work weekly. I am fasting during Lent eating only fruit, milk, whole cereal, nuts.

March 21—Janis didn't come in because of storm blowing her road shut. They came in later- and Davy is sick unable to keep down his food or milk. She called the doctor and he said let him starve and give him six drops of paragoric. So we did. Davy still very sick but kept down medicine mixture. They left at noon...

March 30-

A-Sin—Moses

1-Ten Commandments are contradictory to Law of Love-mainly speaking

2-1st commandment is Law of Love, Sabbath relative

3-Moses judged severely not by Law of Love but by Law of Mankind-Law of Justice.

B-Trinity

1-All creatures that are created are given free choice

a-No such thing as sin until made by man.

b-Man chooses the road he follows
c-He names the rules
d-To be of the Law of Love is to be free
2-The Law of Love stated is- God Is

C-Christ's forgiveness of sin-
1-His meaning—Karma
2-Sin is your agreement that you have done something wrong

D-God's definition
1-Hurting another in name of God

April 3—Palma's baby born about 11:20 am. 7lbs.—Kenneth Grant. She called me up. Her letter talks of her wishing to nurse baby and having trouble with cracked nipples—of baby having to be made to breathe because they pulled him out. Of her stitches-of Kermit being excited about holding baby. Of baby's good nature until circumcised. Trying to get second hand buggy. In other words Palma has become a mother.

[Below is Mother's life reading of Self. This is the first of her life readings. These were an important part of her past life therapy.]

April 13—

1-My first realization was as a bit of pollen being dropped down into the flower-to become new life.

2-My first response! God is, I am.

My first question. I am, where is truth?

This became my evolutionary thread-but also the knots in the thread...stumbling blocks to progress.

3-Original agreement—-God is, I am.

Definition of God—-God is—rest is manifestation.

4-My pattern of evolution—-

As plant, decide to be one celled animal, as low form of animal decide to be higher, up thru fishes, reptiles, mammals elephants, anthropoids, man.

First twenty eight man lives—-untouchable—live only year or two, decide "death is way out".

Twenty ninth life—experience Christ's death on cross and His drawing all men to God and decide, "Man is redeemed by love." So now everything that happens is limited, colored by—subconscious thought of what is truth—and love must rule—Response is to throw out Beauty, Music, Ceremony because they do not fit my definitions.

Found freedom in dying for truth.

Found guilt in breaking with love and truth. ie; (war, murder breaks with love—ceremony breaks with truth.)

In this present life—consciously sought God—December 1948—"God, I want to find what Jesus found." From there on began giving up free will.

"Thy will be done"—four and a half years.

"Love is"—prayer for two years

"Beauty is"—prayer through music almost three years.

Now, "God is" prayer . I say God is, I am, Where are these? To be whole I must say "God is." When this in my understanding can contain, I am All— then I find All in God—God in All—and am not longer separate as individual creation but go back to All, adding something—

The ability to do and be the Will of God—This is as far as I know or comprehend at this point.

April 20—[Definition of E, as in e-sessions.] E is that creative force that always keeps God (union with God is) before us and always works (within the range of our will) to help us reach it.

May 31—Sally stopped for help. Jan and I talked together of infinite choice and infinite freedom.

June 2—Palma and Grant [my 1st born] arrived at three.

June 4—Palma helped repaper wall that leaked.

June 6—Recital-[She names nine students, and the people present including me.]...Janis played waltz by Chopin—Alice her first piece in public—Fur Elise. [Janis had been a music major at college; Northern Michigan College.]

June 27—Jan and I met tonight and I feel that it was one of the more enlightening of our sessions—We started out with our opposite ideas of sacrifice—She—that man must sacrifice. I—-that sacrifice is not the way. We were asked to count from 1—-16. These three found it. [the way.]

*1—Krishna when he heard a bird sing he experienced the joy and music of the Universe.

*2—-Jesus saw that God loves each of us and the only thing we need to do is to seek to love God and seek to be open to His Love.

*3—Lao-Tse saw, heard, felt, "everything"—not just what he wanted to see, hear, and feel. Therefore he had full experience. [Then she lists other of the sixteen whom she says] "thought they found 'the way'...

I was interested in these three because they were always part of the "team" when she worked with you. I think she saw these as having reached the "Godhead".

June 30,—I am told to pray for the next step- so I ask about steps to Union.

1-Choose God supremely
- a-Give all I have
- b-Go where He tells me
- c-Pray-Thy Will Be Done
- d-Total Obedience

2-Obedience
- a-Prayer hours exact
- b-Fasting-food, time, rest, drink, pleasure

3-Love God , man, self
- a-Erase all in way of Love
- b-serve in love with love for love
- c-Receive Love, beauty, truth

d-Give up hatred by letting love and hatred flow thru me.

4-Love is a prayer-every thought word act given for the Glory of God

5-Union-

a-Open to All

b-Experience expansion-electric ecstatic fully All

Aug. 18—Move today into *role of Prophesy*—Elijah—"In those days shall Elijah come forth from the wilderness and teach the sons of Man, lest he destroy himself." In October the role of healing.

Sept. 2—Yesterday picked berries in swamp with Clara and friend.

At this time Alice is in negotiation to sell store building to Lester Passinault, Jeweler.

Sept. 8—Expected to hear about selling store today—not heard yet at noon. Jan coming in for afternoon and evening.

Sept. 12—Still wondering about the store—because I'd like to remodel north end of kitchen and get new sink and have house painted this fall yet, but presumably God knows what He is doing since He is handling all my business....I feel at loose ends—waiting for arrival of Palma, indefinite, and business with L. Passinault indefinite....

Sept. 25—Letter to Palma. Never have I felt the tears so close to my eyes or the lump so big in my throat—Our visit seems to have been incomplete. Your happiness is so dear to me, your future of my very fibre, but still I am very grateful to you both for coming. I have washed dishes, swept, picked up, drunk the rest of the coffee, put the books away, and found one small pair of socks which I enclose....

Grant and I had come for a visit and during the time I was there, I had a two month miscarriage. It was with mixed feelings that I lost that baby. I was heartbroken on the one hand and also relieved as two children so close together would have been overwhelming, not to mention that by now, I was realizing that Kermit's drinking was a problem.

Sept. 26—Have been in prayer for Kermit since he came home soused a week ago last night. Thursday night Edna, Helen, Janis and I got what was called a life review as we sat in Edna's car down by the dock looking at lights coming across bay on the water. It reads something like this.

Kermit's genius is the finding the point of contact between Spiritual Reality and Physical Reality. His lives for eleven centuries were given—-...In this life he also comes to the end of feeling [that] he can find it in study of science—... My prayer for him has been to absorb his guilt of murder, and torture which shuts off for him all idea on possibilities of evolution of the soul...

Nov. 14—Palm came with Grant...Grant came to me and laughed aloud for a good ten minutes as we sat before the fire. He is most friendly—and wherein they say babies are sober and solemn, he gives one the impression of happiness—pleasure in everything he does—He works very hard at play, learning to climb up to standing position, walking around objects, and practising for hours sitting down. [This was my good-bye visit before I left for Southern California where Kermit had taken a job. Thus the following sad entry.]

Nov 29—Dear Palm, again I am sick with lonesomeness for you and Grant. I went down to Brynhild's and let her talk, then snoozed thru a

Grant in California

roller skating race. Would like to have stayed thru the evening but she was going out, then later having company. So came home and cooked two onions sliced in that meat broth that was left—built kindling fire and sat at rollaway table to eat it—then practised and now sit with an indescribable emptiness.....I feel just like the day Janis left for New York only worse because I had you to come home to then—Wish I had a good book to read—or Janice Taff were home, or someone would drop in. You on the other hand are full of eager anticipation.

1961

January 1, 1961—Have been in Tucson since Dec.26 for event of birth of Bridget Ann whose birthday is Dec. 22. First few days rainy and cold—then clear skies and warm days. Lyn took boys, Rae Lynn and me into the canyon for a ride. I let a car bump me as I entered left turn into the freeway in El Rancho shopping area. Very inconvenient time over New Years....Bridget Ann (august and lofty)—(St. Anthony) is a lovely baby—pretty –strong—sleeps twenty hours a day—up during the evening till eleven sitting the rounds by laps. All the children seem to accept the baby.

Spent Christmas week with Palma. Janis and baby are starved all the time. Still no car to use. Paid ten dollar ticket fine at traffic violations court—Margaret took me down and we stopped for lunch. [Lyn and Margaret are friends from Mother's year in Phoenix.]

In retrospect-May 8—[about January]-Janis soon began to take over her share of work....The weather was ideal and the children loved me and responded beautifully. Alvin was grateful but even so I began to feel in the way about the third week. Palma and Grant came down the fourth week I was there and I enjoyed the nice feeling of our being together. Tredway visited parts of two days. [At this time Janis lived ia a small two bedroom house so it was pretty full with five small children and four adults.]

Went out to desert one beautiful afternoon and watched the reflection of sunset on a mountain. Had chicken dinner there which Lyn cooked and talked briefly with him. Margaret says he no longer suffers those terrible headaches since Jan and I ran off his birth pain....One night we ran off Bridget's birth—found she was aware of each person's soul and the only break was where they took Janis away from her. Her choice in this life is to Glorify God in all she thinks, says, and does....

Owen and RaeLyn were elated at my coming....When I got there RL & O were out to meet me—David didn't wish to be disappointed . When I get inside he felt me all over to see if I was real. Then hugged and kissed me for several minutes....

It was sad parting when I left—Jan was not nearly as strong as she thought but I wanted to spend time in Phoenix—Margaret took me there to Gordons. [Psychologist from Phoenix days.]

For six days I was in misery running off that which for him shut off truth. Then Sat. night I worked with him on the "shut off" for full flow of truth and love....

Even Helen [Gordon's wife] allowed me to help her forgive me. I attended their prayer meetings [Mormon] and was allowed to contribute—Helen made me feel very much at home....

Had my best time at Frances'. Experienced 'Aum' when working with her. Enjoyed her diet of raw fruits, vegetables and nuts and sunflower seeds and homemade whole wheat bread made with freshly ground grain. Every morning we walked two miles in the field before breakfast—this is very much my style of entertainment—Then I read 'Autobiography of a Yogi' in between walks and talks and meals and prayer and working with Frances to run off her fears and resistance. I also like hearing her humor with her antique shop customers. [Frances, Gordon's sister, was also a friend made during her year stay in Phoenix in 1951-52.]

Written May 9 about Feb. 2—...Kermit picked me up at Disneyland Hotel—Showed me yard and house they had rented while I was away—First four days went well. Visited Beckman's plant [Beckman Instruments where Kermit worked on Spectrometers] and watched Spectrometer, $97,000 instrument in operation drawing with red fountain pen vibrations of samples same as I had felt when working with Yogi. Science and religion may be as close as contact on electric switch right there waiting for someone (Kermit? By his choice) to throw the switch.

Kermit also took us up and down a mountain wild and wooley. He had previously seen a mountain lion there and tracks were still clear.

Palma's baby came the 7th—.Eric. [Eric was my only baby that came early. I was sure it was because of all that jostling riding in a sports car over that wild and wooly mountain the day before.] Mr. H. (Palma's guardian angel) [Here mother is saying that Eric was Mr. Higbee in his previous life.]...He is a lovely baby. But from 7th on my stay was so unpleasant with relationship to Kermit that even with the pleasure of serving Palma, Grant and Eric, I counted first the weeks, then the days till my leaving.

...He ended up in jail and was really angry when we didn't bail him out, but he had borrowed $170 which left me short for my fare home ....(He was) picked up by the Sheriff drunk. They really treated him rough and it was a harsh treatment and experience for a gentleman and he was glad to get home. Grant reacted everytime K was late by banging up chairs, toys and TV. He's really fond of his dad—even though I feel his dad disciplines him army style, for disciplines sake. Palm and I worked almost every night he was out to release him from despising and judging himself, to release him from hate...she was helped greatly by regaining her perspective and sense of humor and hope—She was able not to be hurt when he came in late and learned thru insight and wisdom how to handle each situation.

While there I enjoyed the lovely yard, the mockingbirds, sound of roosters, crows, sheep, fig tree, the poinsettas, hibiscus, orange, prickly pear, century plant in bloom.

We also spent a week-end at Tredway's new home. [My cousin who now lived in Santa Maria, CA.]

Palma got four teeth filled in his up to the minute [dentist] office. His house built California style around garden set up for gracious living.

In retrospect; Gratitude for Palma's

...maturity

...graciousness

...humor

...natural gentility

...beauty and grace

...sweet motherhood

...easy relationship with Sally, Kermit, Mother, neighbors, friends, Larry

...friendship and love and generosity

...quietness, honesty, good housekeeping, cooking, managing

...good companionship.

Gratitude for Eric coming into our family with his giving and receiving love strong enough to win Kermit over and to harmonize family.

Gratitude for Sally and her modern approach to life.

Gratitude for the month with Grant and being able to win his affection, confidence, and get to know the interesting person he is and his response to life.

Letter to Janice Taff enroute to L.A.—American Airlines?

I get the feeling from this point of view how we see things in perspective. Two hundred miles to right we see Pike's Peak. 14.000 feet high looks like an ant hill. The mountains we rode through and under by train or over by car which awed us so completely are mere erosions from up here—Hoover Dam? A child's dam and lake behind it but a snow puddle that comes boot high as he wades through it. Maybe that's how our unscalable problems look to God.

The jet glides so smoothly, you would not know it was going at this tremendous speed. You can keep the coffee in the cup and not spill it. Below, over New Mexico, red flat with cliffs (red) and dark purple plateaus in the distance the snow purples and peaks blues and whites so that one can not see where they meet. Far to the right the blues are so bright that they appear as a vast lake with snow covered islands. Albequerque appears as a domino game.

This cabin is pressurized and I don't feel the discomfort but a little heady with a strong mixture of oxygen supply automatically; masks are presented for each passenger,

There must be a cloud layer beneath us. It looks like Munising in winter. Pretty patterns of pure white stuff tinted with pink and gold and shadowed with blue. They gave me a perfect seat for viewing. Window just behind two right engines. You can really see river formation at this height. The teeniest crack lead to bigger cracks which join others until you see the canyon and broad river itself. You can also see what Lao-tsu says about the quiet strength of the force of water.

Now below are brilliant reds and yellows where the rocks, mountains contrasted by dark charcoal grey. Of course, even as I write these words we have crossed New Mexico. We took the southern route because of high winds west of Chicago.

Out of Chicago the neatness of the layout of the farm country was striking. The purple my art teacher used to have us mix would be perfect for these mountain shadows and canyons.

We had perfect lunch preceded by martinis and hor d'euvres. I took tomato juice. As you know I'm afraid of becoming more uninhibited than I am.

When I see habitations in this apparent wasteland I just wonder what attracts these people…sun? ...minerals? ...freedom...or a combination? Oh the gorgeous teal blue river cutting through the rockland that is plum colored with blue black shadows. Every ridge curving every which way consists of the color brightness and its shadowed contrast… the same old story of opposites, paradox, and the secret of God's beautiful arts. Tusquehela River——below a tiny village at the foot of a mountain and reservoir of water as big as the village. Those straight lines cutting the desert must be RR tracks. Now we approach peaks as we pass over a desert town.

Gee, when I think of pioneers crossing stuff like this I don't wonder we're a strong nation....California coming up!!! [I included this letter because it was such a nice description and gives a taste of mother's writing skills.]

At this point, I am diverging from the journals to go back a little into her family and life on the farm. I found this letter where Alice talks about her life on the farm as part of a letter of gratitude to God.

April 8, 1953

Dear Father God,

This is going to be fun; but not quite fair, since you know the whole letter before I write it, having instructed me to do so.

First of all I want to say thank you. There are so many of them, but each is tremendously important—

—the wonderful mother you chose for me,

—the sensitive and keen minded father,

—the farm I was brought up on,

—and the pigs and their pink babies,

—mother cat and all her broods of kittens she cuffed and loved into beauties,

—[the cows] Bess, Daisy, Jenny, Kippi, Gold and Silver; Latitia called Pet and Hoosier.

I must diverge here. These cows taught me so much of appreciation of animals. I remember so well how George and I would go after the cows over the pastures through the cow trails. We took Sport, partly for company and partly because he enjoyed it as we did. We'd go to the top of a hill and say, "Listen," and he'd stop his dog-panting for several minutes and sit perfectly still without so much as breathing. We'd listen for bells, then we'd have to listen for which of these sounded most like our bells. It was fun to decide which bell was which, Jenny's, Daisy's, or Cherry's. We could tell them more by the particular shake of that cow's head than by the tonal quality of the bell. Jenny's was an even, determined shake, Cherry's violent, Daisy's quiet, Bess's even and motherly. Those cows had cow-ality, (personality I reserve for persons.) Kippi always was at hand looking for that bar of Fels-Naptha soap. How often it disappeared before she came right into the shed to find it on the wash table. That was candy to her. Cherry could not be tamed, always insisted on Cherry's way. Daisy was just an ideal cow. George's cow we called her. Mother always gave us the calves. Pet was my cow. She licked me while I milked. Jenny was steadfast and sensible. We never needed to be aftraid of her long horns because she used them so gently, like the day she tossed Charles out of her path by his overall straps. Hoosier, an imported Jersey bull, made ours a real herd. I was always sorry that my father feared him and put the ring in his nose. My mother was not at all afraid and he was always gentle with her.

I have always been glad for our cows. They added much to my knowledge, understanding and enjoyment of life. It is a pleasure to know the various tasks connected with churning, bringing the cows home from the pasture, up through the long shady lane. We had such a lane once. It was always poetic to see the cows come through at sundown, and leave shortly after sun-up.

I never accepted the pigs while on the farm, but since I have experienced Grant Woods painting of the pigs and yard, I fully accept them and find them as beautiful as any other animal.

There was a baby rabbit we caught, half white and half brown. One of a mixed brood, apparently wild-tame. We treasured this but he disappeared and we suspected our cat....

I am glad that my parents believed in education, permitted us to attend school, and encouraged us to learn all we could. Perhaps I am even more glad that I didn't go until I was older, and even then spent one glorious winter on the farm without restrictions. The day we discovered the logging road open and slippery with a mile of hill. We slid the whole day with an exhilaration unmatched by any later thrill. The scolding my mother gave us for the worry we caused her did not dampen the spirits of that ride-climb-ride, and its accompanying companionship. I would not trade it for any year in grade school.

But grade school had its moments, too. All of them add up to what I may become: The evening I walked home in April, feeling-watching-hearing-smelling-tasting-touching (rather being touched by), the promise of spring as I followed the course of the streamlet through the mud down the old wagon-wheel rut. That is the time that I wanted time to stop. I wanted it not to discontinue. I wanted nothing to change. But the hour passed from afternoon to evening and I knew Mother was there at home waiting supper for us. When at last I arrived I found home-made biscuits and fresh sweet milk and a two-quart jar of blueberries, and love, much love. I realized then, as now, that one enjoys each moment, moment by moment....

We played house in the swamp. It's a wonder we didn't all die, drinking that swamp water; but we didn't. Maybe someone forgot to tell us we would so we didn't get to thinking about it. This was at recess. Another recess that teaches me much was when the teachers enjoyed playing ball so much with us they continued right through to closing time. Here the unexpected use of time was more valued and more keenly remembered than any lesson could have been. And we learned. We learned keen joy, sportsmanship, equality with the teachers. [We learned] fairness, and by the way we all felt, I suspect we got rid of much pent up boredom from just lessons. Also the programs we worked on as on ART were very productive to character building. Through these we really learned to love school and our teachers. We practiced at school, we practiced at the town hall, we made soup in the wash boiler and had lunch together. We curled and braided and brushed one another's long hair.... Our pranks were neither unkindly nor dangerous, but were very frustrating to the teachers. One I always laugh at the remembrance: Our teacher, a very young man, always walked his beautiful girl home from the post office where they met each day at lunch hour. This made a very happy nooning for him. This day we rang the bell early and he ran the half mile back to school only to find we had played a joke....

[She goes on like this about her whole life, much of which we have already covered, but I wanted to include this first hand account of her early years.]

Another thing I thought I might include is some letters from Grandma the last years of her life. She was still out west with Uncle James and the letters describe their life in the late 50's.

Westfall, Ore.
Feb.12, 1957

Dear Alice and Everybody,

James received your letter today. James: Thanks a lot for your help with the birth certificate. I needed one if I were to get a job with Douglas Aircraft, but I never heard from them yet. I received a letter from the Bureau of Public Roads saying I am eligible for the job, and they wanted to know when I would be available so I am sending the forms back to them so I will probably get a job with them soon. We may take off to California soon as I will be close to where they want to send me. I think that I will get on as I will be ahead of the college boys as they don't get thru until June and the Bureau of Roads needs to start work ahead of the contractors.

Wish me luck. I haven't found as good of people to work for here as I did in Marquette and Munising. I hope the Birth Certificate doesn't cost too much. We got a letter from Jack from Peru. We are all OK here. Hope you are the same.

Love, Mom and James

Orleans, Calif. General Delivery
March 19, 1957?

Dear Alice and Family,

Here we are at a new address again. We left Sacramento last Monday it was an all day drive but we made it.

This is a town of two hundred population in the NW corner of California up among the high mountains. I think it must be the Coast Range. James applied to the Bureau of Public Roads for a job and they sent him here. So he went right to work for the next day. We are staying in a hotel here and there are no motels. So I have nothing to do but write letters and of course make the beds. I guess I'll be pretty lazy if this job lasts all summer.

There is a wide river running very fast downstream so I can watch that for amusement. There is a lot of nice pines all over the mountains too.

How are you all? Rae Lynn and Owen must be a lot of company. Are you still in Munising, Janis? How is the weather? Getting warmer I hope. It's kind of chilly here yet with the snow on the Mt. I hope you are all well and happy.

Love, Gran-Mom and James

Orleans, Calif.
August

Dear Alice, Palma and All,

Well I'm rather lonesome for a letter from some one so I'd better get busy and prime the pump.

I've been alone this past week as James has been working up in the hills too far for the Bureau to haul the crew so our men folks have been gone since Monday. We expect them back tonight tho. (Sat.) Where we will be going or what they will be doing then is anybodys guess. I have good neighbors here tho they tell me all I have to do is holler and they will come running.

I haven't heard a word from John and Madelyn in a long while so I don't know where they are. Last I heard he had a job from the Sacramento, Water something. And all he was doing then was sitting in the office doing nothing but drawing his pay. But they likely sent him somewhere by this time to work.

I went with my neighbor to an Indian PowWow the other night. They were dressed up in the Indian style with feathers in their hair and were dancing around the fire. It was pretty good. There are two Indian tribes around here that I know of.

Sure hope you folks can take time off to drop me a card soon.

Love, from Mom and James

Orleans, Calif.

I received your most welcome letter yesterday. So as to my being disappointed at your not coming to see me, I sure would have liked to have seen you. But I wouldn't have liked to have you roll down one of the ¼ mile banks to get here. The roads from here to Willow Creek were not very safe at that time of the year. Willow Creek is the closest US Hiway 45 miles away. James has been working on this road and they have improved it a lot since then it was quite slippery at that time. The roads are good now tho; now that it is dry.

James is working for the Bureau of Public Roads . He is in the surverying crew and has some hard mountains to climb. He got a sore foot from climbing yesterday, so is laid off today.

Orleans is right up in the Coast Range Mts. About 50 miles from the coast at Eureka. We are quite aways away from Irrigon, Oregon and I don't hear from Myrtle. I wrote, but so far haven't got an answer so they might be up in the area harvesting, and not have time to answer. She is not very quick at answering anyway but I know her troubles that she is nearly always very busy. I guess Mary [Jane] is going to college this summer so that takes money too. She might be able to help out next fall tho.

Yes, we have a little movable home of our own now so it just costs to park it, about $20 a month; not too bad. We went 90 miles to the coast at Eureka to find a trailer hitch but they didn't have one so will have to try again sometime. It gets pretty hot here in the daytime but cools off at nite. The cherries are ripe now. I bought some from a farmer at 75 cents a lb.. Wish he would come around again.

Did John and Madelyn get to Munising yet? Last I heard from them they were going there and Limestone. Hope they had a nice trip.

Hope you all have a nice time together this summer.

Love, from Mom and James

2014 Chestnut-Apt 5
Long Beach, Calif.

Dear Alice and all

How are you all? OK I hope. We've really got summer here. Not too hot and not cold. Nice sunny days and cool nights. There is some smog but it doesn't bother one much.

We went down the ocean road to see Aunt Mary at San Diego. She and Ed were both home. She is in a wheel chair and can walk a little if she holds on to the chair. She has a hard spot in the inside on one side and it hurts her to raise her arm. She has suffered for so many years but still keeps up. Jack and Madelyn took us in their car and they all seemed to enjoy the visit. Ed is as strong and healthy as ever which is a good thing as he has to do all of the housework and cooking. He was in construction so he and Jack had a lot in common to talk about. James is not feeling very well yet. He has been looking for work and got one short job. They nearly always say they won't hire men over 49 years, and he shows his age. If they are too old for work, the gov't shouldn't take so much out of their paychecks without paying them interest.

There seems to be a lot going on here at Long Beach so guess this is as good a place as any for work. Well the mail man is due now so guess I better sign off. With love to all of you from all of us.

Mom

Jim: [Myrtles son] We went and visited Grandma's sister in San Diego (she was an invalid, and they looked just like each other!!) Her husbands name was Ed and he was 6 ft. 1, a great big monstrous man and he'd pick her up and carry her and set her down in a chair and pick her up and put her back in bed. He'd cook and clean and give her a bath. That was when I was 16, 1952, Grandma was living with John [uncle Jack] and Jim [uncle James] and me and we travelled all over the place. We travelled all over from construction site to construction site and I'd always get a job. Every place we'd stop we'd work. Jim [James] wouldn't get a job so he wouldn't get nuthin' to eat. John and I would get first pick and when we were full then James could eat whatever was left. Grandma rules. She was tough. If you didn't work you didn't get nuthin'. Grandma would take all the money from James 'cause he'd just blow it. He'd buy strangers a drink. He'd just give everything away.

Palma: Uncle James was a dear old soul. He came and spent Christmas with Sally and me out in California in 1961. It was shortly after Grandma died, I guess he was lonesome.

Shaver Lake, Calif.
Fall 1958

Dear Alice, Palma and Janis,

I just received a letter saying I didn't answer your letters. I'm sorry if I neglected you. I thot I answered them all but I might have thot one out and didn't write it. I guess I'm getting absent minded in my old age. Well, I'll try to get this in the mail anyway.

It's pretty cool here today and feels as tho we might get some snow, but the sky is clearing a little in spots. Guess we don't get much precipitation of any kind here anyway, at any time.

Jack and Madelyn

I had a letter from Madelyn saying they were coming down the 26th of this month if all is well. [Aunt Madelyn wanted Uncle Jack to be called John so Grandma was respecting that here.] John had been away for some time but he is back home again last I heard. We went to the fair at Fresno last week . There was quite a big doings there and a lot to look at. One could walk around all day and then not see it all. Fresno is quite a big town about fifty miles from here.

I see in the paper that there has been snow in the passes already. This place is close to 5000 ft up so guess we can expect snow any time.

Is Janis still in Munising? Is Palma away at college this winter? How many more years does she have? I hope she finds work that she likes when she finishes. James is still working on the Bureau of Public Roads and will be there until snow fall and then I don't know where. Will let you know when and if we get located.

I just got back from the town a few minutes ago where we get our mail and groceries. Are you coming west this winter? I hope we can get to see you if you do. Well best of luck Alice, and love from Mom and James.

Shaver Lake, Calif.

Dear Alice

I wrote this letter sometime ago. Since then we have moved but we are still in Shaver Lake. No wonder you don't get my letters if they get lost in my writing paper box. We are living in a house now so have plenty of room. Must get supper now.

I received your very interesting letter and sure appreciate your thankfulness. Hope I don't forget to mail this in the morning.

Love from Mom

It was in December of 1959 that Grandma died. Janis says she died of bladder cancer. She was 81 years old. She had lived a long and adventurous life, the last 20 years or so following James around to find work. Now, back to the journals.

June, 1961—Elijah: "And in those days shall Elijah come from the Wilderness and teach the sons of men lest they destroy themselves." Which brings to mind the words of the song, "If we build our own castles and bomb them away, we shall be our own judgment on our judgment day." ...Understanding of Elijah as given June 19, 1961.

1-Elijah accepted as Son of God

2-Elijah given thought force

3-Elijah in contact with thought of Heaven and earth...

4-Elijah given healing for those who desire it

5-Elijah given sight and insight

6-Elijah transmuted from Time to Infinity

7-Elijah given complete and perfect health

8-Elijah given telekinesis, teleportation, clairvoyance, and prognosis when needed.

9-Elijah given readings on any person needing help

10-Elijah released from self

11-Elijah emerging from individual to Union

12-Elijah living "God is."

13-Elijah living "Man Can."

14-Elijah hearing music of Universe- "The Great Silence."

I think that Alice believed that she was to take on the role of Elijah and called herself Elijah. Therefore she felt this responsibility to keep the "sons of men" from destroying themselves.

"Man Can" became the title for her manuscript of her beliefs and philosophy which I recently self published.

At this time she is also exploring her ideas on "choice", which in her therapy, she believed to be really important. Hers being "God is."

On a more mundane level mother is spending this early summer sprucing up the house by painting and getting ready to sell it, it seems. Also gearing up for a visit from Janis and I and our children at that time. Janis came with her four children by train from Tucson. Then I came with my two boys so there were six children under seven years old. From the sounds of the journal, it was a rather troubled and hectic visit which ended mid-August. I was having trouble with Kermit and had had thoughts of leaving him. Janis was also overwhelmed with problems of her own.

> Journal entry-no date—"I still haven't done my sheets-have a terrible time with my emotions concerning the children being gone—not to come back to this house by present plans—(will sell late in Oct.), and gone so far. I need strong motivation to do simple things like sending left behind things, painful to wrap, and wash bedding and sheets they used and wash off fingerprints around house. It is like divorce facing me with old way of life which I have found so pleasant.

She wanted to let go of the house for many years after, as it was an old house with a lot of upkeep, but it also held safety and many memories. She ended up living in it until she died.

Here's a poem that was published in an NMU art publication. She wrote this in the later 60's about the conflict she had concerning the house.

WOMAN'S EYE VIEW

You said, "I'm glad to leave this house for you
Here among the lakes, hills, trees
You've always called heaven. You'll never freeze.
Your fire will keep us both warm, Love." Yes, though

You left me prison bound. I never knew
How deeply ingrained your spirit dwelt within
Each column, each beam, satingold, built in.
The polished birch, the patinaed bronzelamps are a clue

To your undented solid selfhood, woman's-eye view:
God on earth. The distinctive rough brick,
Its well-fed blaze, speak surely of your worth,
No less your love-full husband's hold: Two

Made one. Please take back the keys. I confess
A wish to be about my Father's business.

Jan. 11, 1962—[Jan's] Baby born today @ 10:30 AM. Alvin called this evening . Her name not given yet—She is fair of skin and hair like Eric, not like her brothers and sisters. A saint. Her birth choice, to give of herself to All. Her nature, reality, her gift to family, reality. [Katie]

[Here's an example of Alice working on herself but it is how she worked on others also.]

March 15—God is working on me this week to heal breach between man and God (in me.) I think the basis for this break an interesting story. Time…54AD. Place? Have only the following facts to indicate place Brown people with black hair and black eyes—Sun (God)—? I seemed to be Indian fakir—ie trappings of cobra, flute rope that we now associate with this. I was court magician, priest, astrologer, fortune teller (male.) Was doing fine, had all people believing in my tricks, was not too scared of cobra but really concentrated while doing this act lest I slip and cobra forget for a fatal moment—-when a concubine of the King came in the middle of night with knife on the place of my heart—and threatened to cook up some charge if I didn't make a poison for Prince's (his son) sweetmeats she was giving him for his birthday.

I complied—for fear of being fed to tigers. Later when son's sudden deathly sickness revealed a plot, I was faced with a five man "tribunal." If I could look them each in the eyes without wavering, I was innocent—which I did. To make a double check, a man eating tiger (hungry)—was loosed in my tent. I also looked him in the eye and he walked away. I was deemed innocent by man but was left alone before God with an aching conscience. I chose never to kill again and although I was a soldier and went to battle forty times, I always was killed rather than kill, down through these nineteen centuries.

This guilt has remained through every life since and I'm embarrassed to look directly into anyone's eyes. This has always bothered me not knowing why I couldn't look directly without embarrassment. Here is the breach. I felt God judged me (in reality He didn't), I judged myself. I was not punished, therefore I continue subconsciously to self-judge. Herein I am now working for the clear conscience that I might once again be able to look mankind in the eye and feel the Genius of God. Perfect non-judgment. Father, eleven saints, Mary, Frances, and Martha are helping me to erase this self-judgement that has followed me through the centuries ... Boy didn't die—but easily could have, save for the potion the King had me make to save him!!

March 31—Got out birthday package for Grant. Spent from 9-2:30 with John [Severson-Clara's 2nd child] while Clara fished on ice. Making up fresh batch of yogurt. Need to fix wicker rocking chair back which fell off. Pick up cleaning and gift for Rae Lynn and vacuum.

Sally and John, Clara's children

April 11—Left home at 11:30 and left car in Esky [Escanaba]. Flew out at 3:20 PM. I had 1½ hours in Chicago. Alvin picked me up in Tucson at 9:30 PM. Kiddies happy and on good behavior on my seven-day stay. Played *Für Elise* in Janis' recital. Jan and I had early morning mountain walk… arrived Thursday at Gordons Foundation….Worked parts of three days at office, receiving Gordons Life Reading….

May 1—[Written while at my house in Fullerton, California. My cousin Sally Severson Hooton also lived in Fullerton at that time.] Sally came to lunch this day and stayed most of afternoon. Palm and I did very little. She set my hair. We had charcoal-broiled hamburger by Kermit for supper. Larry [Hooton, Sally's husband] stopped by after class to see me. Kermit bought '54 Ford from Maurice today, $185—

May 2—Grant came into bed at 6:30 this AM to get the picture straight about my leaving. He wanted to make sure I was going home, not anywhere else. Palma's good bread for breakfast. Have been eating her fig jam and pomegranate jelly.

May 19—[Back home]…I have some questions for you, God. Today when I should be rejoicing because you have promised me wholeness, beingness, I am unhappy about the subject of Validation and Invalidation. When I asked the Trinity, they answered they would absorb my invalidation at which point I realized why I am bothered about it. If I am to prophesy and speak for you, then I must understand this Element Time. Do you speak in "Time" or only in "Course of Events" as you have taught me? When you say "Immediate" do you mean this hour, this day, this week, this month, this year, this lifetime? "All" answers; God is, and we are a part of his glory.

There is always the matter of Choice involved in all parts of each event. Since God does not Violate Choice, He does not Violate Time, so "Course of Events" is usual pattern. Time only relative. When God says "Immediate" He means basic Choice and "now" Choice of parties toward the certain event made in the direction of that event, or the choice in this affair is, "Thy will be Love." He can, for example, say any specific date for me if it does not interfere with choice of other party. He can arrange the course of events if all parties say "Thy Will be Done" concerning these events....

Further instruction—I must learn Beingness. ie—Just "be", as Janis always says she needs to "be". Concerned not with events in time, but just "I am that I am." God is—and experiencing this glorious fact every moment....

As I read through the rest of that year's journal, I can picture Mother practicing Chaconne for next weeks lesson. She was very frustrated by her music lessons but kept them up as she was determined to learn the piano better. Her students really benefitted from her teachings. She seemed to take the students where they were, and used her creativity to take them where they needed to go. When she started beginners, they came every day and by the end of a couple of weeks they were really playing. One of her students was not good at sight reading at all and so she got a book that was easier than the girl was able to play and had her play the easy book slowly, in time, without repeating anything. The student became very adept at sight reading. It was easy for students to come either at noon hour or right after school, since our house was across the street from the Munising school (Kindergarten to Twelfth grade).

Brynhild, Edna, and Jan Taff, continued to gather for E sessions. Most of the time they would meet at Alices' on Monday evenings and sit in a circle in front of the fire, using the fire with its many faces as fuel for their symbols. At one time this year, they decided that these sessions would be given to All (rather than placing specific people in) for their direction and duration.

As summer arrived, Clara and Ole took mother out to the Kingston Plains, to pick blueberries, sometimes finding them lush on the bushes and the blackflies biting and pesky. She sent some to Owen in Arizona for his birthday. Evening walks and talks with Brynhild were one of her recreations and watching TV at Brynhild's or Clara's would keep her from being lonely. [Alice never had a TV in her home.] Lake Superior called and she would walk splashing along the edge of the water enjoying the sparkles on the water, sometimes taking a swim, if the water was not too cold. Other evenings she played Scrabble with Helen V. after taking a picnic out to the beach. She was good at just picking up a basket with a few items and making it a fun outdoor meal. Many entries in her journal said, "Went out to Rock River today." Or—"Enjoyed sitting before a fire with Edna at her cottage today."

None of these activities quelled her prayer and meditations, though. She was very actively seeking "clearness" of her psyche by working on her spirituality and looking for blocks to "free choice." She spent much time counseling those who needed help, both friends and family, and always was praying for their healing and her own. Always grateful, mother was working her way towards her "career" of spiritual counseling of others.

Janis was still in Tucson, Arizona, and I in Fullerton, Calif. Mother and I wrote each other about every two weeks. Mother often wrote Janis and I long letters on her typewriter and sent us carbon copies. That way I knew what was going on in Janis' life. I also wrote her letters of my woes, and she would send me back symbols and empathy.

Love, Love, Love

EARLY IN THIS YEAR Alice felt she was ready to share her knowledge and wisdom. She wanted to write a book about her experience and although she was excited about doing this she also had hesitations about the publicity and notoriety this might bring. Keep in mind that in the 1960's reincarnation was a very novel idea. So, as this year progresses, so does the book.

> **Jan. 7, 1963**—…Working to heal an integral reason break. (Fall of Adam story.) When we "choose" to be men, we automatically choose reason, which is analytical thought, which shuts off intuition or integral thought or Faith by its very nature. It causes the break in Man and the realization of good and evil. Didn't begin writing as I had thought—still get "January".
>
> **Jan. 14**—Letters from Janis and Palma. Janis has been up to Palm's and Tred's with just David—who had a good time with Treddy and Grant and was no trouble….
>
> **Jan. 23**—Last night as E Group was" putting in" the ones we wished to help, Palma called and asked for help, so we put her family in and I continued through night to absorb her charge against K, which was preventing her from getting well quickly of the "flu"….
>
> **March 2**—I find my dreams have taken a new turn. [I] can solve all insoluble problems in them so I don't have to wake up after each impossible one. [I] can climb out of, off of, dangerous places, play pieces so they sound like music, and eat unpalatable foods; even how to cook and serve them given in dreams.
>
> **March 12**—Letter from Palma—Sometimes I get to feeling, in spite of my disbelief in divorce, and my belief in K's basic worth, that Palma is paying too highly trying to wait out K.'s immaturity.

There are places in this 1963 journal that I see, labeled; copied from "a page a day." In these parts of her writing, there are areas of her journal sidelined with red ink. These seem to be some of her work on MAN CAN where she was writing a page a day. Some have to do with her "muses" or entities she uses as guides. Some have to do with prayer and philosophy. Pieces of life readings show up in these areas also.

Also at this time she is communicating with Norman Cousins, long time editor of *Saturday Review*, who she is hoping will help her publish.

In August I see her add "An Invitation to Mankind" which will become her subtitle to MAN CAN. On that day it appears that Krishna, Christ, and Lao-tse are her guides.

Speaking of using guides, the following excerpt from Jeffrey Duvall's book, "Men, Meaning and Prayer" talks about her use of guides and Jeff's experience in working with Alice.

> One of the important personal openings to this teaching [of finding his personal format for prayer] came to me in my thirties. My yearning informed me of a desire for guidance and the need to complete some confused and broken experiences left over from my twenties. In moments of silence I openly called for support and found myself returning to the land where I'd spent most of my twenties——the upper peninsula of Michjgan and the shores of Lake Superior. Shortly after arriving in Marquette, Michigan, I bumped into an old friend and elder, Hilda Rasmussen. Hilda invited me to go the next day to visit a friend in Munising. I agreed to go and immediately felt my body react with a vibrating, anxious sensation.
>
> We drove together along the shoreline of Lake Superior. The power of the lake as a great natural source added to the anxiety in my body. We drove into Munising, an old fishing village that formerly had a lumber mill that supplied frames for Model T's in the early 1900's. The house of Hilda's friend was a simple structure, but the minute I walked in I was hit with the scent of something true, the smell of evolved eldership. At the head of the dining room table sat Alice Tredway. In that moment, when our eyes met, something happened in the room. A silent, reverent energy, charged and condensed, overwhelmed me. Upon later reflection, I came to see it as a fluctuation in time that transported me into a largeness or compression that shaped lifetimes into moments. I was not afraid. After a short while, I returned to normal experience as if falling through many levels of reality to the earth, and landing in a realm of pure love. All of this had happened during introductions.
>
> I knew intuitively that I belonged nowhere else but here, with this

woman. A part of me that had lived long ago, that had known and embodied a deep profound way of living had been contacted. My meeting Alice Tredway brought this awareness to me instantly. I had heard of her when I lived in Marquette those many years ago, but I was not ready then. She had the reputation as a tough medicine woman who had been helping people find their meaning and purpose for most of her seventy some years. In her medicine work she helped people align themselves with their personal life destiny. Her upbringing involved wild crafting and foraging for food in the forest. Her family lived in a small cabin and heated with wood. Most of her time had been in the outdoors. In her mid-thirties she received a series of explicit dreams that she resisted for many years. The dreams, as she described them, had the vividness of waking consciousness. She could literally hear and taste and see the full range of color and touch as if she were physically experiencing the dreams. The dreams told of a shamanic practice that wanted her to bring it forth as a way to guide people into soul evolution. Alice called the method "The 24 Steps to Godhood[Sonship]." She believed each of us had come to life many times, over and over, on our path to Godhood, or what she called evolved humanhood that endears us to divine compassion and love.

We spent the day telling stories and partook in a healing prayer circle that had been a part of Alices's practice all of her life. I gave Alice a massage, having completed a program in massage therapy. When Hilda and I stood to leave, Alice looked at me with her mostly blind eyes and said, "Come back and work with me." It was a clear invitation, the significant moment my body had prepared me for earlier. It took five months for me to arrange another visit. In the depth of winter I returned and spent twelve days alone with Alice Tredway. We worked every day. A morning session and an afternoon session. She put me through her forum. I have pages of notes from this compressed time with her that packed, in a few days, years of teaching. The details are less important. The essence is, Alice Tredway helped me reconnect to my spritual, soul support system, something I had once known and operated out of but had mostly lost. Alice called it, "Having your team."

She would sit in front of her fireplace at the beginning of each session and ask the question, "Who are we working with today?" She always lined up her team, never worked without first assembling her soul support. Then she looked at me, or more correctly, sensed me, given her state of near blindness, and asked out loud, "And who is Jeffrey's team Who are his helpers?" In silence next to the fire's radiance, we waited. Then again Alice asked me directly, "Who is on your team?" Images, entities, archetypes, beings spirits, whatever they wished to be called began showing up. These helpers were the team that would always be with me and help me through the challenges and difficulties of my life. She taught me that Spirit, at least in part, is there to assist us in finding our meaning, purpose and loving. She was strong about asking for the team to show up, and giving thanks to it when it departed.

She had a unique perception of Spirit and the spirit team that assembled for any given period. Things would be going along, apparently quite well, and she would suddenly say, "Okay, we're done. Spirit has left." And that was it. Or she would say, "Our team is gone," and we would end the session. Often, the factors that most contributed to her saying this appeared related to the level of ego present. As soon as someone began to think it was he or she, and become attached to his part in the healing or insight, Alice could sense the way it squeezed out Spirit. It's strange to consider that, as much as she touched me, I still resist her teaching at times. I forget—-which is one of the most common forms of resistance—and let myself drift without inciting my team to support me. Having experienced the fullness and peace of the team, it is amazing that I would ever leave it behind, but that is what happens. And so I have often said, as much to myself as to anyone else, that a prayerful life, or a life of faith, is a process of remembering, and often remembering to remember. It is a practice of developing second sight, as the shaman have described it, that nudges us back to the awareness of our sacred truth. It's almost as if a member of our team, or maybe several, are given permission, or asked, or assigned the job of reminding us. They might say to us, Remember what you said? Remember who you found yourself to be that time in the sweat bath, or when you heard the poet read, or that moment in a particular dance when a vision came to you, or the wisdom of the desert during a solo fast? This prodding to recall who we are, to renew the practices that feed our yearning and connect us to our meaning, is to me the essence of a soulful path....

Greatness is very normal. It is often quiet. It is not about dominion over others, over the earth. Greatness is about losing ourselves in the wounds of all nature, and coming to rest on the true virtues of love. As Mozart said:

"Neither a lofty degree of intelligence nor imagination nor both go together into the making of genius. Love, love, love, that is the soul of genius."

Alice Tredway was blind, but she held the tails of her ancestors and invited others to find their meaning by grasping with their trunks her strong tail. She gave of herself fully and did not allow false fears to diminish her contribution. She knew and lived the genius of which Mozart spoke.

Sept. 6—...Had a fantastic dream this morning—Debate—I took the affirmative chair—Leslie [her old college (boy)friend] and Gordon [psychologist from Phoenix] my worthy colleagues—Issue: "That Men are free who stand in God." Other: "Men are freer who stand on Reason." It was a huge audience and I stated our side and Leslie defended and presented our side brilliantly—was so surprised to see him there and to find him on my side—Gordon argued persuasively—Our side won all affirmatives and won over most opposites. Beautiful building for worship built by audience...

Below is an example of how mother worked with people at this time. This is the outline "given" to her. This is a person who had various physical and mental problems.

Sept. 7, 1963—God's purpose and plan for her:
1-To receive and give love.
2-To accept, receive and live life.
3-To forgive past and present relationships.
a-husband last life
b-A D
c-B and N
d-her mother
e-herself
4-To learn the real nature of charity—to give without recompense.

His(All's) first assignment. A twelve page letter to Father[God?] "Telling Him Off."

Sept. 9—M [H G's sister who stayed that summer at Alices' house] and I got eight baskets of pine knots for fall fires—on lovely plains road—leaves beautiful...

Sept. 18—Clara called today at eight—to go look at blackberries out to farm. We left at nine and found coloring beautiful—striking, but blackberries frozen. Stopped by at marsh but blueberries also gone. Another summer has just closed for me and autumn begun.

Oct. 24—Filled our baskets with pine knots. I have decided that gathering pine knots is my favorite sport and one we enjoy a second time by the open fireplace. Both Janis (letter) and Edna called my attention to Oct 12-Saturday Evening Post article on Teilhard Jesuit Priest—book review and summary of his life. Book: Phenomenon Man-*Evolution Godward.*

This is a letter she received from Norman Cousins of Saturday Review. It was the beginning of a correspondance that they carried on through the finish of her manuscript. Since she was not receptive to any editing, the possibility of her publishing her manuscript with Saturday Review fell through.

Miss Alice Tredway
June 27, 1963 115 E. Chocolay St.
Munising, Michigan

Dear Miss Tredway:

I was moved by your letter, and by your evident concern for the future of mankind. As you indicate, unless we take deep thought on our situation and match our actions to our thoughts, we will have failed ourselves as well as mankind. I deeply appreciate your willingness to put yourself at my service, but I must say in all humbleness that I defer to your own judgment of what needs to be done in regard to the problems you list. Your own concern is so patently sincere that I am sure any action it dictates will be constructive and meaningful. I'll be most interested in knowing what initiatives you intend to take. Again, my thanks for your heartfelt and inspiring letter.

Best Wishes, Norman Cousins

March 6, 1964—Outline of book came thru today and I find I have already written up material for most of it. Wrote Janis for copies of summer effort, so I can mark them up and save the original intact. There are to be three drafts altogether.

May 13—Put my first manuscript into the mail today. Dedicated to the Star of David. Acknowledgment—Eternal Gospel and Prayer Partners. Title and Theme—"Man Can."...

May 22—Just received my first rejection slip from Fred Wieck, Harper and Row, and have, as Krishna has taught me, experienced fully the pain, the disappointment, the disillusionment, the discouragement, and the sadness, that "man can" but won't....Later after two hours of doping, felt release and wrote him...that man can but won't.

Doping was one of Alices' terms. A name for sleeping off "unconsciousness" for release from unconscious blocks in the psyche. She believed that when she received negative energy either of her own, from past lives, or from others that she was working on or for, she could let that energy pass through her to All, for healing her and/or others.

May 30—55th birthday. Janis sent a sound tape of... family including a song made up by David, "When the rain comes, the cutworms come out, when the sun comes, the mockingbirds sing." A story read by Owen, "Clifford my big red dog" and piano pieces by Rae Lynn, with Janis playing Rachmaninoff...

At Georges [next day] with fresh Lake Superior fish caught in the morning by Clara, and cooked by Clara—cake by Lois [a cousin]—potato salad by Alice—ice cream by Clara and coffee by Loraine. A perfect day.

June 18—...Manuscript needs revising. Take out identities, need for proof, ambiguous phrases, add four life readings—Mary, Peter, Stephen, Christ, John?...[These entities were used as valences (viewing from another standpoint), and as guides for Alice and for others. For instance, she always told me to ask Peter for help. He was my guide and seemed to like rebellious natures. When working for Karla, she would advise me to ask Mary for help as she was a guide for particularly vulnerable souls.]

June 21—Read through my manuscript. It inspires me each time and would especially if I were reading it for the first time without the wonderful experiences that produced it. Called Howard Brinton and he told me where I could send it....[Howard Brinton was an author she met at Pendle Hill. , One of his books was "Early Christianity and Ethics."]

Uncle George turned this farm (he and James bought it for Grandma in the 40's) into a Motel in early 50's and this farmhouse became his family's dwelling but also a wonderful restaurant. Located near Escanaba it was an excellent gathering place for family occasions.

June 22—...When will I ever arrive at [the] point; all that matters is to love God Supremely?...

June 25—Wrote NC [Norman Cousins]...asking him to read manuscript; for his response...

June 30—Nice letters from the girls—also one each from Rae Lynn, Owen, and David. Will frame RL's crayon drawing of "Horses" which I think is a treasure. Wrote Janis and Palma and sent Rae Lynn's birthday card out.....

July 4—Went to parade.....I went out to Camp 7 on a different road. This time cousin Lois there. [Last time she went Uncle Charlie and family were camping with Clara and Ole.] All waterskiing. John successful. I tried and succeeded. Broke up camp. Had a swim. John [eleven at the time] rode with me and we came back still a different way. Had a malted at Charlies with John...

Uncle Charlie, Aunt Jackie and first grandchild.

July 8—...Letter from Jan. They all "fit" in red Land Rover and they "plan" to come.

August 5—...Just got into bed and I heard "Alice" [and] Rae Lynn came in and hugged me. [Rae Lynn was 9 that year.]

August 7—Janis washed and I baby sat. Breakfast and downtown for caps and ten cent guns for Kate 2[years] and Bridget 3[years]. Clara's for fish dinner.

August 9—Out to the farm and found raspberries around stone heaps to make raspberry pies which Janis did today for supper....We spent a day with children and Alvin at Kingston Lake beach and were able to swim but Owen became frightened of open lake and couldn't be coaxed in....Owen (8) enjoyed working with his Dad and uncles on sidewalks and liked the woods. David liked the chipmunk and being back here but soon got lonesome for his "bigger world" in Tucson. Rae Lynn (9) was happy and right at home. Katie (2), loved the water, berry picking, the beach, the woods and especially blueberries. Bridget (3) was not at home here but liked staying at Reff's. I didn't seem to mind the noise and confusion this year, was amazed at washing and cleaning that had to be done each day.

August 28—They were off [for home] bright and early. We cleaned up kitchen and left for Rock River. [We being mother and Rae Lyn. Evidently Rae Lynn was staying for a while in Michigan.]

Sept.11—Kermit called and said Dr. Smith doing exploratory on Palma. 1/2 hour later—burst appendix 5 hours past. Prayed "support" between 1st and 2nd call. Then "took poison" all night and day...called [e-group] for help.

Sept. 14—Edna and I worked taking "abortion?" all session....I called again and Palm said "I'm going to be all right, mother."

I was newly pregnant at the time and that was why they did the exploratory. They thought maybe it was an ectopic pregnancy and the fallopian tube had burst. We all supposed I would lose the baby. I didn't. I was fed intravenously for 5 days, kept on morphine to keep my system quiet and healing, and antibiotics to fight the infection that was throughout my abdomen. I came home and Sally helped for a week or so 'til I got on my feet. Many entries in mother's journal about her and others praying for me. Being newly pregnant, I was nauseous, weak from the loss of weight and sickness, and sore from the incision. We were all grateful to Sally for helping with the two small children and the housework.

> **Oct. 2**—...Had the experience last night of spending the night in the woods unexpectedly with Clara, John, and Rae Lynn. Could not find our way out of the many hills. Slept under Hemlock [tree]. High wind twisting about and cloudy. No compass, matches. We couldn't hear town sounds and road sounds until the wind subsided this morning. We set off just as dawn broke in direction of traffic sounds. Walked up and down steep hills with no paths and thru watery, slippery swamp. We were a bedraggled crew—walking two miles up highway at 7:30-8:30 and no rides offered. Had only light wraps to wear and it rained three hours!! This will be, in time, a treasured experience and Rae Lynn says, "We had an adventurous day and night." John made funny jokes all night—no supper—no water or blankets or fire. A hill in middle of virgin forest, with good company. Fifty degrees with wind and rain.
>
> **Oct. 12**—Palma writes her incisions are better, but still nauseous. Grant doing extrordinarily well in school and she proud as punch.
>
> **Oct. 17**—Mailed book to Pendle Hill Publishers.
>
> **Nov. 15**—Just before going west. Finally found enough money to get to Tucson. JY sent $100 and LY $50 and Janis $50 which gives me one and a half tickets to Tucson, with $20 left for traveler's check? Pat offered to loan me money for the trip. At first I refused but now I have accepted because I need to pay on heating oil, gasoline bills, water, groceries,

and dairy before I go. Can't feel right leaving town without paying even though my way is paid by Lyn, Joe and Janis.

Nov. 16—In foulest possible mood. Decided to write book as novel, starting at point of publication and getting criticism etc.

Nov. 17—Wrote to Simon and Schuster concerning manuscript. Copied p. 50-51-52 for them.

[At this time Alice and Rae Lynn flew to Tucson.]

April 29, 1965—Read Palma's letters from Lansing, Monroe, Fullerton, 1957-63. Her letters remind me of my mothers; a light touch but give a comprehensive picture....

April 30—Today read Jan's letters from New York City. They are...serious, philosophical, deep, and lonely. Well worth re-reading.

May 1—Still staying in to hear phone...[I'm expecting Willy any day.]

May 8—Palma called this am. Had her third boy at 10:30 am her time. Kermit just now called at 4:00. Said he'd just seen her a half hour ago. [Kermit stayed at home with Grant and Eric.]

May 9, Mothers Day—Called Janis last night and she had heard from Palma. Called her to congratulate her on her new boy, Kermit Warren II...[Later renamed Kermit Will, called Willy.]

May 30—Halstead reunion at George's Bayshore Motel. [This was a big reunion that I didn't get to, but I have pictures which will give you the flavor of the family at this time. All the brothers and sisters were there and many of their offspring.]

June 17—...Called Janis and they had been trying to get me. Katie is sick. Doesn't like the desert. Want's to return [to

Brothers & Sisters *(l to r)*: Charlie, George, Jack, Clara, Alice, Myrtle, James, and Tom

Brothers *(l to r)*: Tom, James George Charlie and Jack

Michigan]. I received her and Janis thru me to All—for Life Force thru the night. [This is the kind of thing that mother did a lot. I guess you'd call it a type of prayer.]

June 18—Hope to get some wintergreen berries to send to Katie today. Brynhild and I walked the...beach...and on way back picked wintergreen with berries and sent them on to Katie, airmail-special delivery. Katie was discharging blood and matter thru nose and returned to normal temperature....She, Katie, carries berries around all day and keeps them in refrigerator when she sleeps. "They are too precious to eat," she says. "Are we going to visit Alice and her nice big woods?"

Wrote NC [Norman Cousins] answering his letter received last Thursday. I still can't figure out from my letters to him why God has me write him....

Aug. 20—In prayer-Gratitude only-for credit, for friends, for such a lovely house and firewood, for piano, for HK, for flowers, for Clara, for blueberries, for sunshine, for the promise that I may love All supremely....

Aug. 21—Clara was scot free after Ole went to work and John to State Fair so we picked berries along...beach. [Ole worked at the Munising Paper Mill and when he worked afternoons, mother spent quite a bit of time with Clara and John.]

Just found out; Emerson—[who was reincarnated, mother believed as] Isaiah, Thoreau, my mother Martha, and now Katie. Now it is easy to understand both whereas before I understood neither. Janis reports that Katie regards blueberries as her favorite food. It was Thoreau's and Mother's [also]....

Oct.10—Watched part of ceremony of Pope Paul's Mass given in Yankee Stadium. Feel no passion for Rite and Ritual. I feel they are just going through the motions and have no idea of Reality of Direct Contact which I have in prayer each day—real ecstasy, warmth, fire, passion, and exceeding gratitude for what He has done for me.

Oct. 19—Jack Brown [Edna's relative] moved from his Rock River cottage to Shelter Bay leaving it free for me. Now I must decide to sell my house now or stay the winter and sell in spring....[This cottage was unimproved—with outhouse, no insulation, and no running water. Her idea was that she could improve this cottage and stay there until the end of her days. This was not the Braamses idea. They wanted to keep that cottage as part of their family corporation and Bill ended up building on this site in the early 80's.]

During this fall Mother spent a great deal of time at Rock River, enjoying Bill, Gloria, and their daughter Susan. She often stayed at Edna's both with Edna there or with Edna and Byron gone on a short trip. She was helping Pete's wife, Peggy, by working for and on her mother, who was ill. She also enjoyed Mary and Mary's daughter Kate and helped out a lot with the cottages and the children.

Alice and Edna at Rock River

From her journals in late Nov., it appears she became very ill. She was not able to keep down any food for several weeks. Since she believed all illness was psychosomatic she did not go to a doctor. She talks about it being Mrs. N's valence. Perhaps Mrs. N had a liver problem. There were references to her liver but as it became mid-December she seems to have recovered somewhat. She seemed to be sleeping a great deal. [Janis says that Mother had hepititis when she was teaching in Stambaugh and had recurring liver problems.]

Dec. 20—...Package of Rock River maple fudge to Palma, airmail, and letters to Grant and Eric. Still sleeping half of the day. When I awaken and yawn it feels so good. No pain now, but general nausea and not specific.

Jan. 9, 1966—...Today experience release from Mrs. N's valence. Called Janis to tell her immediately...Evaluation Mrs. N—1-Alice will receive flow thru. 2-Alice will be healed...God says; neither success nor failure for Alice, but flow-thru, healing well being, understanding, insight, and NEXT STEP FORWARD!...Three nights...love force to Palma and Kermit on his problem.

Jan. 14—Letter to Palma...Christ suggests to Palma—Ask Mary to help you. Ask Christ daily with your cup of coffee to fill you with enough love for the day for yourself and each family member. Ask that you may receive my love force given for you daily. Ask that you might receive Eric's love and give him love daily. Ask to see Grant and Kermit with love.

Symbolism (letter to P)—1)Tree in Arizona desert reaches tips into ground to grasp every available drop of water—she should reach out for love from Rae Lynn, Janis, Alice, Eric, St Peter, All, Christ, St Mary, David. 2) Family arranged according to love...Eric, Kermie, Palma, Kermit, Grant.

She wrote back—I believe in your work more than ever after that letter. Everything you said is so apt. Just what did you do? Everything worked out so nicely...(I yawned off tension three evenings.)

Jan 19—Peggy called and said her mother [Mrs. N] is worse since I was released from her valence. I feel unwilling to and am not asked to resume this manner of prayer therapy, but asked in prayer what could be done. Answer—Mr. N has temporized with God, has not really given up his religion so does not really have God and the help possible for him. God says his house remains divided. There is really nothing I can do save give whole family to God.

Feb. 8—...Clara's for whitefish livers. [This was one of her favorite meals. I found I could buy them this summer and had some. It certainly reminded me of Alice.] Stayed with John after school. [I am] working on Alice—giving up life and death. Worked for Grant seven hours. Working each AM early—erasing Palma'a revulsion toward K when he is drinking so she can see him with love then....

Feb. 13—...Peggy called. Mrs. N died. Came home to take bath and present family to All....

Feb. 14—Livers with Clara—Then I watched "Harvey" with Brynhild, and found it delightful. Will always remember Jimmy Stewart as Elwood P. Doud, now as well as Lindberg. I identified myself with Mr. Doud and his big Rabbit throughout.

March 3—Letter from Janis who is planning a vacation with Palm next week. She took children on mountain hike and also they (Alv and Jan) took them up to play in snow at Mt. Lemon. Letter from David (8) about trip, and thank you for "nife."

March 13—Today prayer is for Grant. [He was having a lot of trouble with bronchial/asthma like symptoms at this time.] Called Palma and Janis at P's Talked or overheard both visiting together over extension....Then to Clara's for "Lassie" and "Raccoons and Pronghorned Antelope." Walt Disney really makes a good picture.

April 10—Easter Sunday—Off to George's, [the Motel south of Escanaba where he, Loraine, and Marilyn lived] with Clara and family. I tried to talk myself out of it but family loyalty won out and maybe I wanted to see bare ground. We had a lovely day, all in all, with a walk, an inspection of the work they have done since fall, and a lovely dinner of ham and salad (by Loraine) and angel food (by Clara.)

April 16—I think I'll call Palma....Kermit's second offense, drunk driving. His boss bailed him out-$500. He had at last admitted his aberration-proposes to not take another drink all his life. [This was the hope that kept me there those many years. I'm sure he intended that, but the reality was, that he always went back to drinking. If I had found Al-Anon in those years, our lives might have been different, but maybe not.]

April 28—Wrote all morning to Herman Wouk, author of "This is My God." He is Jewish, a Scholar of the Law of Moses. His life-reading shows him to be high level Mankind. 14 steps up Jacob's Ladder. Point of letter: Choose God Supremely. Give up all else, including Law.

April 30—A day of complete frustration...Hal [her piano teacher] came an hour late....He gave no explanation of his hour's tardiness. Also when my frustration increased to unbearableness at Rock River, I suspected the worst. That they do not really want me there but rather want Bill to have cabin. May 11—Expecting Edna and Bill? tonight to work for Bill, what to do with his life....

May 12—...Began today to write, personalities, with no thought of publication. Will receive theme for novel later....

May 22—Bill came at 7AM. Gloria at hospital. We had pancakes and ham together. Then he had a short nap and [Dr.] Olson called to tell him he had a baby boy. [Jack] So Susie had her way again. I went to RR and Edna and I walked west on beach and ran off Bill's emotion in school and growing up—until now....

June 13—Continued writing personalities from Mary's and Peter's view....

June 17—-Continuing writing personality from view of Saints, Trinity, All, Palma...five others...

June 26—Writing personality sketches of those on my prayer list today. JW, John and Jesus…

July 26—…Write Palma. Received pictures of boys and new house and negatives colored. [We had just moved to Rainbow Heights, Fallbrook.] She plans to go up to Sally's this summer. Janis also…..[Sally had recently moved up to San Jose. We did travel north with Kermit. He, Grant and Eric went on to hike the Sierras. Willy and I stayed with Sally and Shawn. Willy and Shawn were just babies.]

Aug.18—Picking blueberries (12 quarts) at Fox River Blueberry area, "burned over periodically by Conservation Department to insure best yield." We found them heavy upon the bush. Large ones blue and black, in clumps, in the marsh. We knelt, sat, stood up to a foot deep in moss and wet, to pick them. No bugs—West wind.

Aug. 24—…I dashed out to Coast Guard…to find berries to send Janis. Three hours picking one quart. So at 8AM today went to Bay Furnace to pick another quart (two hours) and mailed them airmail/special delivery insured. $3.74. Gold Nuggets, I say!!!!

Sept. 9—I just can't make myself do the things I should be doing to get house ready for viewers, not knowing what I'm going to do. No incentive…

Sept. 11—Edna stopped in after doctor's visit. We had a cup of rose hip tea. I asked her about cottage and she said all she knew was "Byron said 'we'll do Alice's cabin next summer'." I just cried. She won't say anything nor will she let me. So now what? God says " It's all set up for you."

Mother's hopes to have a winterized cabin at Rock River must have fallen through here. Somehow the communication was not good and her ideas were not in synch with the Braamses. She was very disappointed. Her friendship with the Braamses continued anyway and she enjoyed staying in various cabins there at Rock River, throughout the rest of her life.

At this time mother travelled west. Lyn Miner came and picked her up and they drove out west together. She stayed at their house and visited with them, Margaret and Lyn, for a time. I would guess from the journals that she came not only to visit but to work with Margaret. She stayed with Janis for a time and visited with her family. Then she came to Southern Calif. and saw my new place in Fallbrook for the first time. Mother always worked with me when she visited. She used the same techniques of symbols, letting me talk, encouraging me to say 'thank you', looking at my situation from others valences, and always encouraging me to love. It was a pretty good visit. There weren't a lot of details about this trip but that's how 1966 ended.

> **Excerpts** from her journal—Came to Janis', to enjoy children. Janis went to Spanish class which she thoroughly enjoys....Walk with M up the arroya then...Janis picked me up and we spent afternoon in Sabino canyon in warm sunshine, children played in icy river....Thanksgiving with Janis and all...At Margaret's last week before Christmas...Two weeks and 3 days with Palm—Kermit fine till last 3 days. He stayed home to rest and be babied by Palm and instead she made me a green tweed coat. Both K and Grant were put out at her attention to me... I wore the outfit home. I had made the skirt and avocado green blouse (wool) and same colored shoes, all very nice....This day as I write in retrospect I find the two months away very good for my soul....

A Prayer: *Tredway -1968*

Jesus,
We've made you so sacrosanct
We dare not follow you across the plank
You laid for us, strait and narrow.
The Brotherhood you offered us, we've refused,
To your sorrow.

God is. This inviolate thought you
Sought to teach us and thus reach a few
Who would choose the Highest Law,
Love the Infinite infinitely,
Become free.

You THREE have accepted this fact,
Had courage to make the pact
With yourselves, God, carry through
To the final Act, Union with All. Bless you,
Trinity.

Several approach the throne, are borned
Up, are not alone, nor scorned,
Though they fear the final price,
Sacrifice, that you affected so bravely that
We might SEE.

Each must pay. Once we choose the Way
We may falter or delay; but there can be no
Retraction of thought or action. Once Accepted,
The Law of Love can only
be obeyed.

Jesus,
You ask me to speak to Man, endowed
With the Spirit of God, help him, proud
Of nature, to move forward to his Goal,
To find his place, his role in Life. Jesus,
Teach me how.

This is the decade of poetry. I remember her saying that at sixty, she learned poetry and at seventy she would take up art. So now she is back in school taking creative writing and poetry with her poetry teacher VandeZande. She's still taking music and also a counseling class. I see reference to a music theory class in her journal. She also changed piano teachers, from Wright to Whitfield and has added violin class to her plate. Every day she travelled to Marquette and attended Northern Michigan University. Talking to her at that time, she'd say, "I'm so tired at the end of the day, all I can do, when I get home, is go soak in a hot bath and go to bed."

March 21,1968—...Turned in ten poems to VZ for NMU paper. [She had several published in both the paper, and the arts magazine.]

June 8—Things crowded up on me. Short story turned out well VZ liked it—suggested 3 or 4 changes to "tighten up" and "clarify" for the reader, which I did June 1st. Wrote several poems that week also ... [one of which is the following.]

Birthday Thoughts

I,

At nine

Sipped the wine of innocence

Fresh from the vine,

Staining dress and lips

With the juice of the wild Grape

Happily

I,

At nineteen

Quaffed the wine of fire, desire,

Played the lyre of youth

Blithely.

I Remember Alice

I,
At twenty nine
Drank deeply of the wine
Of Womankind
Fulfilled
In me.

I,
At thirty nine
Partook of the wine of sacrament,
Finding
The meaning of the firmament
In Christ's love,
Truly.

I,
At forty nine
Accepted the wine
Of non-judgment,
Finding therein
Freedom to be myself
Intrinsically.```

I,
At fifty nine
Taste the wine
Of discernment.
The sips that pass my lips
Burn with love for You,
Most joyously.

Aug.28—Resume of summer events. Janis arrived at Menominee bus depot, 9 PM June 25th- having come by train, bus, and Red [Land] Rover, from Tucson with five children. Owen 12, RaeLyn 13, David 10, Bridget 7, Katie 6. She looked fresh and beautiful. Her 35 years make her look more beautiful. Hair rich, color clear.

Janis' children. *(Back row l to r):* Rae Lynn and Owen. *(Front row l to r):* David, Bridget, and Katie.

Owen—has accomplished much in this life. Shows up well under Janis fine teaching.

RaeLyn at difficult age. Has lost, temporarily I hope, her fine tact she used to use to get her way. Speaks ill to those to whom she should speak most kindly. I took her back to about seventy places in the life previous to this one and we both enjoyed the experience. [Mother said Rae Lynn was my father reincarnated.] She is very advanced spiritually, creatively healing with problems and people. It is disconcerting to find her retroactive at this adolescent point in her life, but she can be sweet…when we needed her to be.

David pleased me especially this trip. He fills a gap in me with his giving and receiving love. Janis was able to do most of the things she needed to make her vacation complete. Au Sable, Marquette, Virginia Hinsula, Rock River for five days, (LaBounty Camp). Climb hill, Tannery Falls walk, Sand Point visits with Lorraine on beach. Pick blueberries, raspberries, make pies, jam, meet VZ, row boat, boat ride to Murray's Bay with Clara, Auditing and E sessions/w Alice and Palma, visit with Bernice—See all relatives, fish fry, trip to Vivian's, visit to farm [at Limestone], visit with [Uncle] James, one week with Palma, visits with Mary Braamse, help Alice get to bottom of music block, understand her problem…, visit with Sally.

Palma came August 8, with three boys. Kermie 3, Eric 7, Grant 9. Got to do many things she wished. Visit Barb and Charlie Stark, Norma and Jerry, Connie Flynn, Connie Gamble, Sally, Edna and Mary Braamse. Visit Rock River four days; Marquette but no ore boats at docks—boys liked others. Beach, help with Kermit, visit to Vivian's and George's. Showed boys Miner's Falls and Castle. Hamburgers at Charlies [Red Cedar Restaurant, and more recently changed to Sydneys], visit Carson and JoAnn, visit Brynhild, fireplace fires, meet VZ . [Mother's poetry teacher, Vandezande, was born the same day as I was, but in Marquette where his mother had to be transported out of a second story window, the snow was so deep, while I was being born in warm Florida.]

Kermie got sick so cancelled plans for Rock River. Alice babysat while P went out with Sally…..Boys hateful this day. Kermit called—Palma/Alice cross. Rock River—slept overnight…..Beautiful day…..Children enjoyed beach all day into evening. [I caught the bus at St. Ignace and flew back to California from Detroit. I had visited with Kermit's family in Monroe prior to my visit in Munising.

A Lively House

IT WAS ABOUT this time that Joan (Tom's granddaughter) came into Alice's life. When I interviewed Joan she gave a description of her experience in meeting mother that I'm sure was somewhat universal, So I'm going to include some of that here.

Joan: My earliest memories of Alice is as a freshman in college. [Joan went to school in Marquette at Northern Michigan University.] She had called me and said she'd like to know me because we were related and I think she invited me to dinner at the University. We sat and talked and I think that led to a week-end in Munising with her.

She was a shock to my system in many ways but particularly spiritually....I had been brought up very religiously Catholic where this was the one true religion...you live life the best you can in a Christian manner and you die and go to heaven or hell. Well, she opened up this whole other world of past lives and evolving spiritually...breaks with your past and resolving them. It was traumatic to say nothing less—and it put me in a state of turmoil. I remember even going to the local chaplain—the Catholic priest assigned to the university— and sitting down and talking to him—I still remember his name—Dr. Webber. To my great surprise, there was nothing immoral about believing in past lives 'cause there was nothing in the Catholic Church or in the doctrine that nullified the existence of of past lives. Also, there was nothing really that stated heaven and hell so therefore all of a sudden I opened this door that I didn't know if Alice was possessed or what!!!

It was so frightening to hear about this, and it was so different than anything I had heard, so when I found out it was ok, I opened up my mind to listen and make my own decision about it.

So I remember my first weekend with her—I'll never forget, she had a little vase of for-get-me-nots. [In her guestroom.] Ever since that time that has been my most favorite flower in the whole world and almost my insignia...I remember her yard was carpeted with these at one time of the year in the spring.

So here was this wonderful woman, so earthy in appreciation of nature, the richness of foods, and her deep spirituality.... There was a longing in my soul for all of these things and the summation of life was all in this woman.

The journeys back into past lives, the beautiful fires in the fireplace, how she'd always start these sessions—"Let's yawn the stress out." So we'd sit there and yawn first. I even think of that to this day when I start yawning, I think about Alice and getting rid of the stresses inside. I think about candles and candlelight—just the quiet solitude of an evening with the fire crackling.

At this time I'm pregnant with Karla, hoping for a girl. In these days we don't have ultrasound so I have to wait and see if she's the girl I'm hoping for. Mother was still very much into her music, poetry and school in Marquette.

April 21, 1969—Joannie came for her birthday April 1st— German Chocolate cake and omelet. Pineapple cheese salad. She has been joining Richard and me at Charcoal Room and Concerts before and after on Tuesdays. [Charcoal Room was restaurant at Northern Michigan University, and Richard was a young man whom mother commuted to Marquette with. I commuted with him the next year when I went back to school.]

Clara allowed to ice-fish. No promise for later. She is now teaching Coast Guard Auxilary Class.

Jan writes of zoning problems.

Palm of Kermit not liking his work.

Sally-selling her second house to move to Alaska.

August 12,1969—Palma called and she is happy. Karla Kristine born this AM.

Aunt Clara at wheel as Captain on Pictured Rocks Cruise Boat in Munising

Mother spent the holidays out west with us, meeting and enjoying her new granddaughter. That turned out to be my last Christmas in California. Kermit took a new job in West Virginia and at the end of the school year, I moved there with the children. Life did not get any better for Kermit and I. At the the end of the next school year, after a particularly hair raising drunken episode, Mother offered "When you come to Munising for your summer vacation, maybe you could just stay and not use the return tickets." That was a biggie for me as she had never offered that before. I always figured I'd made my bed and I had to lie in it. You see, I was afraid Kermit would not let me go if I told him I was leaving him. I'm not sure how he would have stopped me but I was a scared, abused woman. As the following entries show, that is what we did and Mother's life became wrapped up with ours.

June 17, 1971—Palma called-felt her life is in danger. Wants to come home [for visit] now….Called to say coming Sunday….Called to say can't come Sunday—will try for Tuesday-2:47-North Central from Chicago.

Written **August 27**—This summer has been a merry-go-round. No time to write in diary since....**Sunday June 20th**. [On that day] simply rested at Rock River and swept cabin. **Monday**-cleaned as much as I had time for, car and house-Monday night went to George's-stayed over at Motel-**Tuesday**-left before noon [to go] 100 miles to Green Bay airport. Back to Motel with Palma and children. [This was Uncle George's motel south of Escanaba.] Karla came directly to me at airport.

Written **Sept 1**—Janis came the Sunday following July 4th—12 in the house. [Me and my four children and Janis and her five.] Every other day we tried to separate the families by one going to R.R. cabin for day or overnight or on an excursion. The children played well for a day then clashed until separated.

Kermit called the third day and demanded answers [mainly when was I coming home.]—Palma said she had left him so he appeared at R.R. Friday noon, drunk. Came to house that night—got drunker and fell asleep on the floor. Palma and I worked on symbolism until 4 AM. Next noon we took children to Pete's Lake and invited Kermit to join us-he did-and sat apart wishing to be included—Next day we went out early to lake again and he had bought suit to swim and help boys with swimming. Saturday night Kermit worked with us. Got outline on 10 July and sent it to him. He came up again and worked 14 hours.

Shortly again he appeared [at Mother's] to stay a week. Had had an accident-got a lawyer who helped him get off the hook and who encouraged him to find himself. We finished thirty hours. But he continued calling every day or so pressuring Palma to come home, by threatening suicide-that he'd lose his job-and threatening me with divorce and trying to force Palma to file for divorce. At this writing Holy Ghost says:

1-He is a child lost in the Cedar Swamp-going around in circles. No positive plan of action.

2-Unwilling to let Palma have "her way."

3-Suspicious of Alice's motives.

4-Growing angrier, more desperate, sorrier for himself by the day.

5-Failing to say the one thing that would release them all. "I leave it to you, God.

This craziness of Kermit calling and demanding answers went on for much of the next year. This did not make life easy there in Munising. I will not keep repeating that stuff but I'm wanting to give the flavor of life at 115 Chocolay at this time. Keep in mind that Mother's therapy worked when a person sought her out for help but this therapy for Kermit was much like someone being told by the courts that they had to go to AA. She was mandating it.

I'll also include parts of the following resumé that Alice wrote in her journal of the summer. I enjoyed these vignettes of Janis' children so have put them here. Janis and children were there for six weeks or so. She and Alvin were talking divorce. Alvin and Kermit phased in and out, and with all the relationship problems it was not a real smooth time.

> Written **Sept. 8**-Resumé of summer...Rae Lynn at 16—permit to drive, helped on trip both ways—pretty, scrumptious figure, very very warm and sweet to me, with expression of hatred to David (her mother in her last life). She and Palma communed quietly. We drove together for Rae Lynn's day with me to Marquette, shopped for me and Palma and had dinner in Villa Capri. I felt very sad we had so little time to know each other, with 8 other children, upheaval between spouses, and crowdedness. It seemed I could only enjoy her presence.
>
> Owen 15—tall—beautiful face, fair hair and skin. Hair long—"eye for eye and tooth for tooth" philosophy was sometimes jarring but as I had no clashes, it went well... except we did not have time together as I hoped. Again the madness of the situation, Alvin precipitating divorce, run-

ning off his insanity, and the crowded conditions of 12-14 living here at one time, Owen's friends extra, causing late hours. The simple mathematics of trying to feed and bed that many individuals in a house geared for at most four.

David…at a "bad age" 13, trying to "raise" family, causing outbreaks between people one way or another. He and Grant paired off to sleep, but often clashed or buddy- buddy got into trouble together. To me he is beautiful, but I would like to have helped him over this tough time with a session. We had only one hour together alone to pick berries. He got to drive six miles—and we to have supper and some-mores by the fire. I feel cheated not to have had several such pleasures but Kermit's 30 hours paramount.

Bridget 10…took her out to lunch and she said, "Everyone else keeps changing, but Alice always stays the same." I had her observe family of six…from valence of Mary, Joseph, Christ, and Father. She is very perceptive, enjoyed lunch and special attention.

Palma and children in 1970. *(Back row l to r):* Karla, Kermie, and Palma. *(Front l to r):* Eric and Grant.

Katie [nine years old] invited Kermie to join us—we drove to Marquette, traffic terrific. Sunday, no shopping, so stopped back at RR to swim. Then to Averies [a gift shop] to pick necklace of agate. and supper at Red Cedar. Katie is, has been a treasure, most of the time agreeable, tactful with Eric and Kermie and gets along with family. She has my mother's "spit wit" and wisdom, her level headed observations. She did express great jealousy of Bridget, and anger at Eric. She and Kermie played many hours together. She could hold her own at cards and chinese checkers.

Grant [twelve years old] is still unapproachable...intellect would appear to be his choice [over love] but at this writing do not have his reading. He...responds badly in presence of Kermit but fairly well with Palma, and feels kinship with Janis. His response to Eric and Karla has improved this summer. He at this writing is frustrated with school, study hour, and students. Hope to work with him soon and regularly.

Written **Sept. 10**—Palma at first flared up at both Janis and me, but after a session or two seemed to understand what was bothering her and was able to help Kermie, Eric and Grant to understand what was bothering them. Palma enjoyed Janis' children individually and did her part to separate two tribes every other day, taking them to cottage or on excursions, to beach or berry picking. She was under great strain with Kermit calling all times of day and night and coming up at his whim....She has given up whole situatiion to God...and maintains her plan to go to school this year is important....

Tredway, [his wife and children] Elba, Treddy, and Rima spent three days in town, staying at [a] motel, eating dinner with us, or lunch. Elba joined us picking blueberries while Tredway took [some of the] children fishing, and on the Pictured Rocks Cruise then off to swim.

The children picked berries and used them their way. Grant—muffins.

Kermie—pancakes. Eric & Katie—jam. Grant—raspberry pie. Eric—blueberry, sugar plum pie. Eric & Bridget—muf-

> fins. [It was pretty hectic as each of us helped the kids bake and use their berries. The blueberries were exceptional that year]. Eric had luck catching trout on AuTrain River with Tred and Alvin.
>
> Examining myself this summer, I felt annoyed at Kermit for pressuring Palma....I was asked by LaoTse to learn forbearance this summer. This seemed necessary with all the commotion and even physical fighting between children endangering beautiful things in the house. Leaded window of cupboard broken at Karla's birthday party when fight occurred....For the most part I was able to stay apart from the frictions occuring as soon as the two families had been together more than a few hours. My chief disappointment was that I had so little time for each child. The children for the most part responded to me very well....

Looking back at this time, it was chaotic at 115 E. Chocolay Street, to say the least. Mother was protective of her house and the fixtures in it and was unaccustomed to the boistrous nature of boys. Of course all would not be smooth with nine children under sixteen years old in any case but was probably worse with all the emotional upsets within the families.

In the fall I commuted to Marquette to school, taking Math courses that were way over my head after being out of school for fifteen years. With the children in school, Mother watched Karla during the day and oversaw the boys when they got home from school. Mondays were a particular trial as Richard, (whom I rode to school with), had a night class so I didn't arrive home until after the kids were in bed. There was some tension between Mother and I often having to do with child-raising issues. Mother would complain, "These children were awful today, and I think we need to have a symbol session tonight." I said, " Oh OK", but I felt defensive and didn't really know what to do about their behavior. I had been under Kermit's "rule" and hadn't really developed my own philosophy whereas Mother was used to her own rule in her house. Below is an entry in her journal of a discouraging day.

Nov. 17—Grant home from school—sore throat today. Kermie going through dirty word stage—Eric the lying stage—Karla the no nap trying stage.

Nov. 18—Woke up with sniffles which developed into laryngitis by night and back so sore I could not move even to put on sock.

Nov. 25—Thanksgiving—Kermit acts pleasant but is tense. We had a delicious goose dinner with wild rice, and mushrooms. Then napped through afternoon. Palma and Karla had a short evening walk and then down to Clara's with Grant through evening 'til nine....

Dec. 28—Kermit was very pleasant Christmas Eve and Christmas. Clara, Ole and John shared our Ham etc. Children happy and busy with their gifts, games, new clothes... outdoor snowboat...Grant-his airplane engine, Eric-his skeleton. Palma and I tried Ouigi Board but she giggled so much by its action that we made no headway. I had thought of giving it to Eric at the same time that Palm bought one in Marquette because she couldn't resist.

Nineteen seventy-two continued much the same, with my family living in Munising with Alice. She instituted symbol sessions* for the family once a week for family unity. We also tried to have a special outing each Sunday where each week a different person picked what we would do for our special outing.

*Sample symbol session: We are all sitting around the dinner table, myself, Mother and my four children. Mother says, "I'll start. I see a basin and the water is sloshing in it as if someone has just been washing up in it. Palma" I say, " I see an otter playing in a pool of water. Karla." Karla [3years old] says, "I see Willy jumping in the leaves. Eric." We say the name of the next person which announces that we are finished with our symbol. And so it goes around the circle, maybe four or five times. Not only does everybody get the complete attention of the rest of the participants, the idea is to allow these picture symbols to get to the subconscious to release emotional blocks bypassing the conscious mind which resists.

That summer Mother took Karla out to Rock River. The cabin they stayed in was unimproved, meaning it had few amenities. There was an outhouse and Karla had a little pottie in the cabin. They got their water from a spigot outside and had to heat it on a gas stove. The cabin was two rooms. A kitchen with sink, stove and refrigerator. The other room was a living room with a bed on one end and a small inefficient wood stove separating the bedroom area from the sitting area. The living room looked out on a beautiful view of Lake Superior.

People came to visit and to work with Mother that summer and we went back and forth visiting. Meanwhile I worked as a life guard at the community summer program. I was able to bring Eric and Willy (previously called Kermie), with me on the all-day outings. Towards the end of the summer I did decide to get a divorce from Kermit. The last semester at college, I did my student teaching in Negaunee driving sixty miles each way in my newly purchased car. By this time I had resolved some financial issues with Kermit and was able to buy my first car, a 1971 Volkswagen Beetle. I was gaining some independence and when 1973 came, I was able to get a short-term job teaching swimming to 4th 5th and 6th grade students at Mather High School.

Up until I filed for divorce, Kermit gave me some money each month. Mother paid for the house and utilities, and I paid for food, gas, laundry and my schooling. I had to take out a school loan for that last year because as soon as I filed for divorce, Kermit stopped giving us money. One reason I had not left sooner is that he always told me he would not give me any money if I left. I now had my teaching certificate and was trying to get out on my own. I sent out many resumes for teaching jobs. A Math major with a Home Ec minor qualified me for 7th through 12th grades. This time was mixed with happy times and stress.

The week my divorce was final, June of 1973, Kermit was in town, and I was ready to celebrate being free. I went out with friends several times and mother always waited up and worried about me. This was stressful for her as she was particularly worried about Kermit's drunken violence. She became ill and after several trips to the doctor we discovered that she was diabetic.

I got a job as a cashier/hostess/busperson at a local restaurant for the summer and mother took Karla and went out to Rock River again. Her motivation that summer was to relax, take the stress out of her life, and learn about her disease. I'm sure she had mixed emotions when I finally got a job teaching at Fife Lake Schools, near Traverse City. Glad to have her life back and sad to part with her daughter and grandchildren. I was certainly grateful that I was given a safe haven for those two and a half years and a chance to start over. It was also special to build my adult relationship with Alice, learn from her and about her life and work. We had always been friends in my adult years, but after that period we became very close. So in August, 1973, I moved to Traverse City, MI. and it was the end of the "lively house" there in Munising except when we visited. It was just two hundred and twenty five miles and so we did travel to Munising quite frequently.

Six Days With Alice

NOW A NEW era was beginning in Alice's life. She was becoming known in the area as a psychic and also as helping people with their problems. Because she didn't have a degree in counseling and was doing work in a non-mainstream area, she worried that she would be "burned at the stake", so to speak, as a witch. She wanted to have a counselor with credentials to be backing her up. So around this time Allyn came into her life. He was a Clinical Psychologist and he tells of meeting her.

> *Allyn:* I met Alice through the Tibetans. The Dalai Lama sent two Rimpoches to the University of Wisconsin, to help set up a Buddhist Study … so he sent Geshe Sopa and a very old Rimpoche. They hadn't been in Madison more than six months or so and I had made a friend of Geshe Sopa. In Tibet…he personally was one of the tutors of the Dalai Lama. I met him through a mutual friend and I helped him to learn to drive and how to pump gas. When I had conversations with the Dalai Lama the first thing he would say to me was "Tell me about Geshe Sopa. How is his driving?"
>
> The old Rimpoche must have been in his mid-seventies and I heard he was going to give some teachings at a farm outside of Madison. I went to those and Jim Clumpner had heard about him and he was there too. When Jim heard that I had connections to the Upper Peninsula [of Michigan] he went ballistic, as Jim can go. In our talking and Jim and I getting to know each other, Jim said he had heard that there was somebody in the Upper Peninsula that was a very good psychic and was well regarded by people. He said someday he'd like to find out who that was so I put that in the back of my mind. [Jim did get to know Mother, not only working with her but helping her to maintain her house. She was very fond of Jim and he has been active in maintaining symbol sessions since she's been gone.]
>
> Later that summer when I got to Michigan [Marquette], in passing I mentioned that to Melitza, and she was so hungry for

Alice and Allyn at about this time.

teaching she said, "Oh, I'm going to find that person." She found that Alice was in Munising. I was not looking particularly for a teacher. Like your mother has her inner source I've always known my inner source, and that has always been my teaching. I've always been drawn to people who have been on the same path. So Melitza started working with Alice and Alice said that I was supposed to come over there. I made all sorts of excuses. Probably because I was up here such a short time, and I have a lot of things to do and I wasn't looking for anything. So partly to accommodate Melitza I went over and met your mom and I loved her. You can't help but love her, you know? I recognized what a beautiful gift she had. So that's how I met her.

Also at this time people were being referred to her for help, sometimes as an alternative to a psychiatrist. So this one gal, I'll call her C, evidently worked with Alice and while going back into her past lives she got into her insanity. Then she decided she didn't want any more help. C went into psychosis and was hearing voices. So mother asked all her e-session people and Janis for prayer support and helped this lady through her psychosis. At a later time she did work with her again and "finished" the session. That was when she decided she needed a commitment from her clients to a period of time for their work with her so that they didn't get stuck in past lives. I'm not sure why why she chose six days, but that was the amount of time she asked those who came to work with her for. I don't think she inaugurated this into her life right at this time, it was just the catalyst for the idea of her clients making a commitment.

I've been asked if I've ever gone into past lives. It's like this. When I left home, I cast out all my mother's beliefs and started over, as much as one can do that. I talked, read and listened and came to the conclusion that past lives were the only thing that made sense to me about the life after death. But I was still not ready to have my mom take me into past lives. I was hesitant for several reasons. The opportunity didn't seem to be there with four young children and always one of preschool age. Also I was somewhat fearful of the new experience, and also what it might reveal. Then, as friends of mine here in Traverse City heard of Alice's therapy, they were anxious to go and see her.

So in my early forties, I took a friend up to Munising for a weekend, to go into past lives with Alice. When she started working with him she said, "I'm not comfortable taking L into past lives, as the time is so short. Also I'm getting directions from the "team" that it would be better for Palma to experience your past lives as I know I can take her back and get her in and out of your past lives."

Back I went into someone else's past lives. The eerie thing about it was that as I experienced the lives and the occasions that this other person was being shown, it was obvious to me that it was not me I was experiencing. As mother guided me to these places in the past, I got phrases and a perspective that wasn't my own.

Then I started dating a fellow and brought him up to meet my mom. He was curious about past lives, and to be truthful, quite skeptical about them. So the scenario was much the same as with L. She directed me into his past and I again found myself with a perspective and attitude different than my own.

The result was, I got curious about my own past lives. So mother did a life reading. In the life reading were the lives that I needed to experience to help me with what I was dealing with now.

She asked me to go back to each one in turn. The first one I remember I was a young girl and was sitting on the top of a thatched roof. Water was swirling around on the ground and it kept rising. It seemed I was in the middle of a flood. This time it was the me I was used to. Always it felt like me and right now I was feeling really alone and not knowing what would happen. But there was an underlying faith that I would be taken care of. I think I needed to know that my faith was strong and that I would be all right no matter what.

The next life I was a fifteen year old boy and had run away to sea. I was on the boat with all the other seamen and it was exciting. I was all set for a new adventure and against the will of my father had taken this step on my own. It was a testimonial to my rebellious side and my love for the water.

Another life I visited, I was a musician. A violin player who was a travelling minstrel. The important thing in that life was that because it was so easy and natural for me, I didn't think I was any good. It was a self-esteem kind of thing. Like what I did was so ordinary I didn't appreciate my abilities. Evidently others did though, as I seemed to be quite in demand for my trade.

It seems like there might have been another one but these are the ones I have carried with me all these years. The really interesting thing to me was that these all felt like me. Even now this is who I am, a musician, someone who enjoys the water, and a person with a strong faith.

I include this as an example of mother's therapy, how it worked for me, and how my relationship with my mother grew through the years as my respect for her grew.

Melitza and Jim [Allyn's friends] were from Marquette and they were so thrilled with working with Mother that soon they were sending people to see her regularly. The problem was, she was living on Social Security which she had been getting since my father died. It was not enough, especially with all these people coming to see her. Since they came from out of town she often fed them and since she didn't want to leave them hanging in the middle of some past life, she also put them up as guests. Allyn was sending her people from Madison also, and so, with my blessing and encouragement, she started charging for her services. She always felt she was doing God's work so didn't want to charge. The amount that she decided on was one hundred and fifty dollars for "six days with Alice."

People would come on Monday and they would start working a couple of hours in the morning, and a couple of hours in the afternoon. Sometimes they would also work in the evening. She'd say, "You go on out and do some sightseeing this afternoon and I'll take a little rest." She often worked with couples so she would be feeding and working with people all day. On Sunday she would rest. This was not every week but she was pretty busy.

> *Allyn*: Now your mother, the people I referred to her, could be from different traditions. They could be from the Jewish tradition, or a physicist or an atheist or a rosicrucian. Your mother could deal with any of this and she could find a way to relate to them. She had that Gleaner quality, too. I've always been attracted to the Gleaner type. When people ask me what I am religiously, are you a Protestant, a Catholic, etc. I don't respond to that. What I do is I find that I'm drawn to that thread that goes thru all of the great Traditions [which in Tibetan Buddhism is called a Gleaner], and, if I have to say what I am, I say that I'm a thread.
>
> I had already had a background in Freudian psychoanalysis and in Jungian thinking so I was very interested in your mother's use of symbols. I think part of the genius of Freud, who trained all of his clients to free associate with anything that was going on in their minds, was to stop the censoring process, and then stuff would start coming up that would eventually surprise them. Carl Jung invented what he called the word association test. He would throw out a word and you would give the first word or thing that came to your mind. So there's quite a parallel there with what your mother did. But your mother was doing it on a purer or a more primal level with the symbol.

The symbol is always related to something that's been happening over maybe a lifetime or something very deep about where the person is stuck. Her use of symbol I thought was brilliant. It enabled people to start to relax into a deeper part of themselves and then stuff would start coming out, And that's what a lot of psychotherapy is about, enabling people to bypass the conscious mind. To tap into the intelligence that is deeper than thought and deeper than just the intellectual mind....So I learned a lot from your mother, just seeing how she operated and being one of her guinea pigs, one of the learners, as well as participating with her. When she would be down in Madison, I would set her up with selected clients and [friends], and as you know, whoever is there, she hauls them into the process. We did a lot of that.

I sent a lot of people to Alice and many of them were friends, some were former clients, some I was actively working with, some were people reasonably well known in the spiritual community. I was very careful who I would send to your mother. There were a lot of people who I would not send to her. I didn't want to waste her time. I also told people the same thing your mom would tell them, that she didn't do quick readings and that kind of thing just to satisfy their curiosity. I think I was one of her screeners, and I'm reasonably good at that. I know how to screen. So I only sent people who were willing to work for a while. They knew they were going to spend minimumly a few days or more and probably come back various times. They were prepared in that sense. For the most part, they were pretty well educated. One fellow was a physician, head of Emergency, at St. Mary's Hospital in Madison. He was of Jewish background. One was a Nuclear Physicist, who had the reputation of being the smartist fellow who ever came through the Physics Department. A first class scientist. Another an attorney, who was a personal friend of Ram Dass. So I tried to be careful, that they be the right people and a lot of these people almost without exception, have found this very valuable and it'd be interesting to see how these people were affected.

In some ways your mother responded to them the same but she responded to them very differently as to where they were coming from. It didn't matter that someone came from a Jewish background, it didn't matter that they were almost a pure scientist, or somebody was atheist or whatever, she was able to be non-judgemental in her relating to these people and so that they were able to explore.

It was around this same time that mother met Elaine, also a Clinical Psychologist but from Marquette. Again she struck up a mutual friendship where on one hand Mother was working with Elaine, and on the other hand she was a "professional" with credentials who sent Alice clients.

Elaine: Well, I heard about Alice from mutual friends, Allyn Roberts, Jim Rasmussen, and Melitza, and I had never met her. Allyn was having a birthday party for her, out at Middle Island [Point], and he invited me to come. I was anxious to come and meet her but I was also afraid of her 'cause I knew she did spiritual work and I just had some fear about meeting her, for whatever reason. So I went to the party and I did everything possible to avoid talking to her directly. I kept watching her talk to people. At the very end, when she was leaving, I went up to her and said, "Hi, I'm Elaine, and I've been so anxious to meet you." We said a few words and she left. I didn't go and see her for another year 'cause, I wasn't ready…[So she went the next year].

I got a lot out of the [past life] reading and…the past lives we did. This one life she took me to, I was a Tibetan Buddhist Monk. She told me she was taking me through that to work on my acceptance of death. I had accepted life 100% but I think I had accepted death 75%. In this life of a monk, I was studying and studying, I was in the Himalayas, in a monastery... and it wasn't until I was about fifty that I was ready to have students. So I had a few young men that would come, and I would spend time with them during the day and teach them things. We knew when we were going to die. So I knew [when] it was my time to die....We had these little lean-to shacks up in the mountains, up higher than we were. When you were ready to go, I was taken up there with a little bit of water and I just sat there (in a yoga position) in front of this lean-to... meditating. When it was my time to go, (now I had never been exposed to Buddha or Buddhism so this was really a surprise to me...) I saw this little fat man (spirit) floating towards me and he got about six inches from my heart chakra and my spirit just went floating out after him. It was the most beautiful, wonderful, freeing feeling I've ever experienced in my life. I just knew then that there was nothing to fear and it was very, very helpful for me. [Alice often took her clients through a pleasant death experience as a way of accepting death, therefore accepting life.] So that was one life that really stood out and helped me a lot.

Allyn: Now some of the people, for example, were those who had no belief, about reincarnation, and other people had a sense, well there's something there and wanted to experience it. I think it was very creative and part of her genius that she was able to get some essence of a person, frame it using reincarnation as a language, in a way that they could see that what they were dealing with was more than what's on the surface. I'm talking about her life readings and also how that blends into reincarnation. Alice probably took the reincarnation thing in a much more literal sense than I do. I don't think it's important if you believe in reincarnation or not. What is important is that you have some experience and knowledge that life is continuous. That's what's important. I think that through your mothers use of reincarnation language and what not, she helped some people to see a deeper connection.

> Also, from my personal sense, and Alice and I talked about this and she didn't disagree, the truth of reincarnation is not whether I was a chicken ten lifetimes ago. The truth of reincarnation is that whatever you haven't finished with, it doesn't go away in this lifetime. If I have not finished what I have pushed under the rug, it will come back again and again and again to haunt you until you are done with it. Until you get it you have to keep going over it again and you waste a whole lot of energy. You can't grow your gift until you're finished with the stuff where you were stuck. So I thought that that was very effective, powerful, and clever way of getting people to relax and say, "Oh ya, that's what I'm stuck on." A framework to start looking.

I thought Elaine's life as a nun [earlier in this life] was interesting and asked her how that affected her perception of Alice.

> *Elaine*: Yes, I had a committed religious life, I was a nun for seven years. I was raised Catholic and I was never exposed to past lives or reincarnation, so it was all new to me. I didn't know she did this before I went there, and so I think there was some opposition for me because of that, because it was a whole new concept. A year before that was when I left the religious life and came up to this area and I remember feeling that I couldn't go back into a traditional church setting, 'cause that wasn't there for me anymore, but I had nothing to fill in the gap and I was feeling very lonely and I missed the ritual that I had been exposed to.. I would go down to Lake Superior and sit there every day, and slowly my spirit started to get healing from the lake just sitting there meditating. Then I met Alice, which really helped me move into a whole different spiritual place, understanding a much broader spiritual perspective. I really feel like I came into owning my own spirituality for the first time. A lot of that was due to Alice's exposing me to reincarnation and her belief system as well as my own time at the lake and with nature. My spirituality comes strongly through

Elaine at her place on Lake Superior shore

nature. Of course, that was real important to Alice, you know, nature. We'd spend a lot of our sessions outdoors or at Rock River.

One of Alice's clients was Mary Ebert who was also adept at poetry The following poem is her take on reincarnation.

REINCARNATION, A Movie Review- by Mary Ebert

This movie is called the story of my life,
It was written by a genius writer in Hollywood,
Who wrote all the scripts.
Produced by M.E[Mary Ebert]. and directed by M.E.
And the star character is M.E.

I just woke up in the theatre watching the movie.
I don't know how many times I've seen it
But I keep forgetting the ending
So I go out into the lobby where it's light
I ask somebody, "How does it end?"
They tell me and I say, "Oh yes, that's right ."
Then I get some popcorn from the eternal supply
And I wander back into the theatre and pick a new seat
Hoping to improve the view.
But when I wander in the theatre is dark
And I'm blinded for a moment
And then when my eyes focus,
I realize I forgot the ending again.
They said, "when I can remember the story
From beginning to end,
I can go home."

In 1983 or so, Mother discovered a lump in her breast. Because she wished anonymity she went to Madison, WI. to have it looked at. She stayed there with clients she had made friends with. It turned out to be a malignant tumor that needed to be removed. and she chose to have a lumpectomy rather than a mastectomy. Radiation was recommended, but since Marquette was the nearest place to get treatment, she said, "I'm not going all the way up there for radiation."

At that time Mother's health had gone downhill with the diabetes as a main culprit. Her eyesight was failing from complications of the diabetes (diabetic retinopathy), and she had a hard time with the pain of neuropathy. The hereditary back and hip problem also plagued her so it was difficult for her to walk and get much exercise. She sometimes had the digestive upsets she had had earlier in her life, and had lost much weight. She continued seeing people who were interested in finding their center and spirituality, even though sometimes she didn't feel too well. Her work was the core of her life and being. She was doing God's work and those that she worked with were renewed of life and spirit.

But her body was not serving her well. In early 1986 at a check-up, she discovered that a lymph node under her arm was enlarged. So in late April, she again went to Madison, and had that removed. Again she refused radiation as treatment.

I asked mother, "Do you want me to come up and help you out?" She said, " Do Jon and Jeanne still want to come work with me?" These were two of my friends from Traverse City who had been wanting to go and see her professionally, but until now it hadn't worked out. So first Jon went up for four or five days to help her out with her recovery from surgery. She, in turn helped him out with his Inner Source. He says, "We had sessions in the mornings and evenings. In the afternoons she rested and I went exploring."

Then Jeanne went to Munising to help her out. To this day, Jeanne still refers to all the help that she got from Alice in those four or five days.

By now Mother was getting quite weak but Betsi, one of her young friends who came to her for counsel and camaraderie, offered to call and/or stop in each day to check on her. It made Janis and I feel better that Betsi was calling Mother early each morning to make sure she was all right. This morphed into Betsi bringing lunch almost every day, and walking her to the Post Office to get her mail. They were like a couple of teen-agers if you overheard them. Joking and giggling and really enjoying themselves.

Later that summer, Janis's daughter, Bridget came to Munising to be with Alice and help her out. That went well and so as autumn arrived, my daughter Karla needed a project. Mother invited her to come and help her go through her "stuff" and help her organize it.

For Christmas that year, Karla brought Mother down to Traverse City. All of my family gathered and we had a very special Christmas, our last one with Alice.

One of her main wishes was that she be able to stay in her own home. By this time she was getting much weaker and needed to have someone there especially at night, to help her out. She continued

Our last Christmas with Alice.

having clients come and that served both of them well. She had someone there with her and they were still getting her wonderful spiritual guidance.

By February she could no longer work with her clients. I went up each Friday thru Monday and helped set up systems for the week in between as, by then, she needed to have someone cook her dinner and stay overnight. She had a big support system in the Munising/ Marquette area and between friends staying and helping out and the Home Health Care people filling in when needed, we kept her at her home until very close to the end, when she went into the hospital.

This was Mother's life was during these last years. It was filled with interesting people who she helped over their humps, and who revered her for her ability to help them find themselves.

In her last days as she lay in the hospital, "terminal", was the term used by her doctor, these people came from all over the United States to say their good-byes. It was a double room but there was no patient in the other bed. This left a guest bed right in her room. It was really special for some of her out of town clients and friends to be able to "keep her company" by staying over in her room. At this time she was barely conscious, but not because of any drugs. She refused all pain medications so that she could "experience" her crossing over to the other side. It was April 14, 1987 when she made that crossing, five days before Easter.

Her bed looked out over Munising Bay on Lake Superior with a beautiful view of the sunset. She couldn't have chosen a better scene for her ending. And so her last days were filled as was her life, with a stream of people who were seeking themselves and their God.